GOD HELP ME

Steven R. Mitchell

Dedication

Since the title is "God Help Me" let me start with giving honor to Lord and my Lord Jesus Christ for always showing up and giving this desperate sinner a chance.

My brothers in arms, Gonzalez, Crumpler, and Little Bit with whom I trusted my life in body and mind.

To all those who helped me over the years, each one loving me thru the times of reflecting the horrors of war. I could not do without you my dear children, Rebecca, Steven, Daniel, Jacob, John, my little spitfire Jennifer, and my dear Stephanie who has gone to be with the Lord.

Thank you to Tobias Moran for all the research help and support and to my friend and faithful intercessor Judy Doyle.

To my wife Jackie who God put into my life. I know the cost of dealing with me from PTSD to all the health problems with Agent Orange.

I will always love you Jackie with over forty years of marriage we beat the odds of the mission impossible because that's where God operates.

Steve Mitchell

TABLE OF CONTENTS

BEFORE THE WAR

Our family was a large one, as I am one of ten children. I was the second born in our clan of Vikings as some of us called ourselves. Growing up, the same question asked over and over was "Are you Catholic?" I guess the two go hand in hand. Never the less, this same question popped up so much, I became ready to give a quick sarcastic answer that was normally foul and rude. The question always reminded me of our poverty and desperate conditions growing up. Growing up in the fifties cannot be explained or understood unless you link our existence to coming out of World War II. The big war tore up families and fragmented them with huge human tolls and cost. The war was over and the need to go on and forget was the driver. The baby boomers went into full swing with the need to find wholeness in a land of pieces.

The day I was born, I had to go live with my Grandmother for a year or so because my Father was put in a tuberculosis sanatorium linked to his service in World War II. The bonding process never took hold for us. My Father had some issues to work out that included anger, drinking and gambling. My Father worked thirty years in a factory and so many of his paychecks were distributed to poker, horse tracks, ticket pulls at work and many other gambling schemes.

Growing up for my brother Mike and I was very strange, as I reflect back on being raised by a true drunken sailor and my Mother, who can be described as a June Cleaver type with a lobotomy. I never understood my Mother. She was just there but nobody was home. I never did understand why she continued to have children, because Dad was not winning at cards and his picks at the race track were usually out of the money. Dad seemed to be locked into a belief system that his negative lifestyle was going to be funded by his success in gambling. Dad's win ratio should have told him something. Add the price that goes with coming home on a Friday night after work, with various characters looking to take as much paycheck as possible at the poker table. The scene played out exactly the same. My Mom would protest and cuss him and he would just laugh, because by the time it was game time, Dad and many of the other players were already lit. Well, it was time for Mike and I to go to work.

We got our bartender's licenses early as the counters were full of hard liquor and mixes. Our job until the game was over, which many times was sunrise the next day, was keeping the drinks flowing and making sandwiches. Tips varied but we had no complaints. However, we knew to hold the money for Mom the next day. Dad usually ended up with bad losses that resulted in ham and beans, liver and onions and nasty

Braunschweiger sandwiches which should have been a crime if you gave it to your kids. We knew the same hell was going to break through for at least a week. The aftermath of the drinking and gambling losses meant physical and verbal abuse until both had enough and decided to be some kind of a family unit again. This pattern, which seemed to go on forever, was tearing us all apart. The success of my Father's gambling endeavors can be easily measured by the following economic indicators.

My Grandfather rented us a home that he owned because we would have had to have lived in the family car - if we'd have had one. The consistency of Dad's losses would have put us on the street every month, because it wasn't in the cards for him to quit gambling. So my Grandfather cut a deal with my Father, and I believe my Grandfather ended up on top. The deal was, my Grandfather's Mother comes with the house. My first thought was, "wow a relative, I've never met one." This could be good since our family didn't get out much due to lack of transportation and reputation. The reputation part can be easily figured out by connecting the dots of Dad's lifestyle and behavior. This woman that came with the house must have come from a mental institution, because she was nasty, dangerous and completely out of her mind. In some ways, she was in the right spot because the way we lived was close to Atilla the Hun's upbringing. I realized early on there was no conversation with this woman. I never knew her name, nor did

I want to. From the time she moved in, she was known as the crazy woman upstairs. Soon after arriving, on a hot summer evening she came downstairs screaming like all hell was chasing her. She ran into our bedroom, then out the window on the second floor – and was completely naked. Now she's on the roof screaming. My brother and I are standing pat, just watching. The fire department eventually came and scooped her off the roof. That was the last I saw of her. I never asked about her and never talked about her again.

My plate was full of drama and insanity. My Father would get off the bus at 3:15pm each day, walk down the street and the neighborhood kids would run and scatter. Growing up we played war games that involved weapons from long clothes line poles as spears. Our shields were trash can lids and crude swords and knives of choice. I had many primary and secondary hiding spots that were well concealed. I would hide in the bushes rather than run to and greet my Father. I would observe his every move, and in some sort of way try to figure out whom he was. I was in great fear of my Father because Dad was short tempered, and I knew he would not hold back. In one instance in a rage, Dad came upstairs with a leather strap and left welts across my face and body. Dad felt so bad that he picked up a high powered pellet rifle for me. I would soon become the neighborhood sniper. I operated out of the attic window from the crazy woman's apartment. The 18x18 window encasement on the second floor facing the alley and the backyard became my post. Targets were plentiful, as I became quite proficient in killing squirrels and birds. We had a walnut tree where the squirrels would feed, and this became their final meal before execution. This relaxed me and was definitely the out I needed.

I believe my sniper training paid off when I was cracking off rounds with an M14 in the Marine Corps. I was an expert in the Marine Corps and that was a good thing. It wasn't long before Dad needed some money, so he confiscated my pellet rifle and sold it at work. On the block where I grew up, all my friends were Catholic, so I saw the religious hypocrisy first hand. Every Friday at the hamburger joint, they would have a special and I would go with the Catholics, who were supposed to be at a fish house. They thought the rituals and going to confession were a joke, so I looked at it like I'll sleep on Sundays while my friends would go to a church they didn't believe in. Finally at the age of fourteen, my Dad finally had a horse come in. We would move and finally own a car. I got so tired of watching everyone I knew drive down the street in their cars. My Mother's sister would invite us from time to time to drive to her house on the South side for a get together. However, because of the size of our family and the fact that we had no transportation, it fueled the bad blood in the family. Everything seemed to come back to gambling. We were going to be punished for the sins of our Father and Mother.

Luck finally showed up for my Father in a horse race. This win still did not put my Father in the black, as he'd been operating for years in the red.

We had a house built on the East side. I guess we were moving on up. We moved my second year of high school. It was

1964, and I attended Arsenal Tech High School. We were already in Vietnam. Tech had two cafeterias, one for the blacks and one for the whites. Soon, both of these black and white Americans would be going off to war. My brother Mike was one year ahead of me and after graduation, Mike joined the Army for four years. Right at the time of my graduation, I did a quick assessment as Mike did and joined the Marine Corps. I graduated mid-term, and the Marines had just come out with a two year enlistment program. At the time, my thinking was that the Marines were tougher and better than the Army, so I had finally outdone Mike at something. We were always in competition with each other. Mike was an Eagle Scout and I was a street scout. Mike was Captain of the School Safety Guards. Mike fired me from my street corner post for insubordination, as I cussed him out during inspection. All I can remember is that your belt had to be white and the badge polished. Mine was neither, so it was during the writing up process that things got ugly.

Mike took his job seriously and I didn't. I still don't know how his belt was bleached and clean. Mom sure had nothing to do with it. I sat myself down and said to myself, "You just graduated early. You can wait for prom and graduation ceremonies in

May or you can join the Marine Corps and get out of here."

My parents continued to have children and Mike was already in Vietnam. The biggest driving force for me was I didn't want to be poor any longer. I knew I had to go to college in order to be successful and rich. As I saw it, my life would be different – it had to be. I was so sick of not having new clothes in high school. I went to a resale shop with a friend of mind and I found so many outfits I wanted that I took them all in the dressing room and layered them on my body one by one. I wish I had a picture of myself coming out of the dressing room with sweat pouring down my face. I was unable to walk right because my thighs were fused together. This had to be a sight to see. I don't know how long it took to get outside, but I was ready to make a dash with more clothing than I ever had growing up. My clothes were mostly hand me downs. Well, not anymore. I never got to wear one outfit. A store detective dressed in civilian clothes nailed both of us. I thought it was really unfair and sneaky of the store cop. I also blamed my inability to shoplift and steal on my parents, since shopping was such a rarity for us.

The detective called my Father and told him I would be released to him. My mind was racing and trying to figure out a way of escape. I knew when Dad pulled into the driveway, I was dead. I knew the silent trip home meant Dad didn't want any witnesses and I had it figured right. My plan was simple – as Dad would pull into the driveway, I would exit the vehicle and run for my life, and that's what I did. I didn't know my Dad could run so fast, however, I knew it was a race I must win. As this whole mess is coming down around me, one of the things you grab for is to justify your actions. I mentioned the hand me downs, and here is the real scoop on that.

There was a family much better off than us and they had two children - Tom and Jay. Tom was the right match for Mike and I. Jay was huge, so his clothes wouldn't fit.

Well, guess who got stuck with Jay's outfits? My Mother was not a seamstress, doctor or knowledgeable of the world, because something happened to her early on and she threw in the towel. Mom was not connected and most of her wisdom came from soap operas and phone calls from people who had nothing to do either. I just wanted a few outfits that fit and had not been worn by someone else. My father is chasing me now and this is his fault. Truth be told, he hated his own life but decided to take it out on someone else. Logic would scream that this was a long time coming. Because of a series of events at home, I conclude that this is a time to put together a plan for my life. I am highly motivated to change my meager little existence. My parents did the best they could with what they brought to the table and applying whatever they had. There is much I never understood. Now I am so ready for a change. Big change. My calculations are two years in the Marines will go so fast and then I will be in college.

On the front end of all this change, I find myself aboard a big jet, flying to California. Camp Pendleton was my final stop. Transportation always excited me because of my lack of it. Flying in a large jet felt like I had already accomplished something big in life. This would be a bold new chapter in my life, and as the bus takes us to Camp Pendleton, I am overjoyed with the fact that I had finally beaten my older brother at something. Everyone knows that the Marine Corps are far superior to the Army in training, fighting and toughness. My victory was short lived, as the drill instructor's welcome to us was filled with words that reminded me of my Father's anger. I'm thinking these Marines have the wrong guys. We just got here, so what is our crime? We are patriots! Reality soon set in for all of us. We are all nothing, no-good, scum of the earth and worse. I was thinking that these guys must know my Father because they are so much alike. Dad was the best at beating down someone and the only positive encouragement I had up to that point was joining the Marines. I guess I could examine that until the end of time to try and figure out Dad's true feelings.

Let's break it down.

I joined the Marine Corps at the hottest point in the Vietnam War. Our TV worked off and on, so I didn't pay much attention to Walter Cronkite on CBS News. I missed watching the endless supply of Hueys and gunships carrying war dead and wounded each night. The fact is, we needed a break from each other and I didn't realize that our family would never be the same. War takes a major hit on families no matter how dysfunctional a family is. This was my family, like it or not.

Boot camp provided new dimensions of Hell for me and all who participated. Many nights I found myself trying to figure out a way of escape and out of the nightmare. Nobody on the planet that I knew gave me a clue of each day's reality that never seemed to get better, only worse. Very seldom did I do my homework and I definitely failed miserably in my research of the Marine Corps. As I go through each day, I'm wondering why I'm still alive. I came to the conclusion that nobody would believe what happens in the Marine Corps. I mean, who would make this up? The turning point for me, and also when the physical abuse stopped was when I scored expert on the shooting range. I was personally called into the drill instructor's office for a face to face congratulation. No drill instructor ever touched me again, and at that point, I had made it through. Graduation from boot camp and AIT was good in a sense that nobody would ever beat me down again.

One of my friends from boot camp had his parents come in for graduation. These folks were great people, and when my friend got his orders for Vietnam he was devastated, because his MOS was a cook. I apologize for not knowing his name, but much of my memory is gone. I remember he was quite a nice guy and fun to be around.

I remember his Mother would write me all the time.

******

I want to take a moment here and express to my friend's parents and family how sorry I am for their son's death in Vietnam. I must also explain my reasons for turning down your request for me to escort his body home. While in the jungle, I did have an opportunity to see your son and we had a blast. Our only arguments were that he always wanted to be out in the bush, taking out the enemy. I told him over and over again that he was in a good place and what I was doing out there would change him. I encouraged him to stay where he was, but he wouldn't believe me. When I heard what happened to him, I was stunned and angry. I think I pieced together what likely happened. I believe he overcompensated and began playing some very dangerous games to replicate the dangers of combat by tossing a grenade. The problem in the scenario was the mix of drugs and alcohol.

An officer in the bush called me into his hut to tell me the news of your son's death and your escort request which was my ticket out of Hell. I would say most soldiers in the bush would have grabbed the ticket and never looked back. Unfortunately, this jungle and war owned me and my thinking. My judgment was completely flawed and in many rights insane. I turned your offer down, leaving the officer and all of my men dumbfounded. My thinking was, when we came to the area where your son was killed, I would find out who was involved and kill them. That was the best way I could think at the time to help your son. I wish I could turn back the hands of time and honor you with such an honor that you bestowed on me. I needed out of the jungle, out of the war and out of all of it. I am very sorry for hurting you and I ask that you please forgive me and try to understand that I wasn't in my right mind – not even close.

Turning the request down should have sent signals to the ones heading into this insane war that something was wrong with me – something very bad. This war had an unhealthy hold on my life and others. This death grip is not easily explained or broken. I remember when I was Medivaced out when I got

Malaria. I couldn't wait to get back to the jungle. Go figure. I regret hurting them so much, but in reality, they didn't know me anymore. I didn't even know myself. I had changed drastically since we'd met a few months back. This war is what I had become. I had no past and no future. I only knew that the battle was there and for whatever reason, I could not leave it. Is that a valid excuse? I believe not. What was wrong with me? What had I become? Who was I? How could I hurt my friend's family? I didn't mean to! I hope they forgive me. This was a great loss for me too. I miss him even now. I miss his humor. But I know he is with the Lord.

*****

My orders were no surprise because I joined the Marine Corps for two years, which meant Vietnam all the way, because there is no time for schooling due to the enlistment time of only two years. My fate is this jungle war. Somewhere in the Nam is my destination. My tag was 0311, or grunt infantry as some liked to call it. I'm just a fighting machine waiting to be injected into the war so I can KILL KILL KILL. I am ready to go because in 1968 and due to the losses each week, the Marines wasted no time getting us into the fight. My calculations were always wrong, but in all fairness, facts and information were sketchy. It would seem reasonable in a life and death situation, soldiers heading into a battle might be briefed and armed with some war data, especially when where you're going is under siege and heavy fire.

In the Chinook on my first day in the jungle, all the new guys had no clue and no idea about the meat grinder we were about to get dropped into. My thoughts on the way were, "ok, I'll just ease into this thing, figure this out in a few weeks and get a lay of the land." But I was rudely interrupted by small arms fire hitting the Chinook. The enemy had dialed into this sector. It was total chaos inside the chopper. At the same time, the Marine in charge is screaming, "When this bird touches down, you Marines get the hell out of here and run for cover!"

THE HOT LZ

I got out of the Chinook and the in-charge was screaming to run for cover and stay on the side of the chopper that we were in. For the first time, and don't ask me why, I realized I could be killed over here. This was a dangerous place. I was in a war. I should have factored all those things in. But my plan was to ease into the war. Plans don't always go as planned. This one sure blew up. There was no easing into this war for me. It was full throttle right from the start.

So I'm looking around preparing for my exit from the chopper. Imagine me. I'm clean, sharp, canteens full, bandoleers across both shoulders, M16 ready to go, helmet, backpack – let's put it this way, I'm ready. I have everything I'd need for a nice jungle war. The chopper is receiving incoming small arms fire and mortar rounds and the landing isn't soft. The LZ was red hot, as they were trying to take out the chopper. As the tailgate is coming down, I can start to see wounded Marines waiting to get on the chopper, with other Marines behind them. The noise is deafening. The smell is unique. The whole thing is confusing. It's total chaos, but chaos doesn't even describe it. I'm starting to gridlock and

I'm not even out of the chopper. Wounded Marines with their guts hanging out

is literally the first thing I'm seeing. Marines are throwing body bags onto the chopper as the walking wounded are getting on.

I exit the chopper on a dead run towards the tall brush as the chaos is happening. I was so gripped with fear, my legs weren't working very well as they seemed to buckle. I ran into a Marine who'd obviously been in the bush for a while. He was bearded, dirty and bloody. He hadn't been shot, but he was just looking meaner than hell. Here I am, clean and pressed, completely out of my element and here's this gruff looking Marine. I'm trying to process the whole thing and trying to figure this guy out, so I'm definitely scared. Out of fear, I asked him who he was. He told me to shut up and give him some water. I immediately flashed back to basic training where they told us not to share water. Then I looked at him. Then I flashed back again. I flashed back and there he was again.

So I immediately gave him my water!

At this point, I'm in full gridlock. Mortar rounds are exploding everywhere. AK47s and M16s are firing non stop. Artillery is being called in, the whole nine. There is a lot of yelling and screaming. I've never seen this before and never expected to see this.

Eventually, there was a lull in the action. By this time, rapid thoughts have been racing through my mind and I'm really reevaluating this thing. I was so gripped with fear, that I got to the point where I convinced myself that I wasn't even mad at these people. They hadn't done anything to me, so why was I here to kill them. Yeah, I don't want to do this. This isn't going to work out for me. This is just too intense. Maybe if they would have eased me into this war thing, it'd be ok. But for now, I gotta get out of here! I want out. I knew I was going to die here. So I had to come up with a plan. The best I could come up with was a stomach ache, and that I needed to be choppered out. I had it all planned out. I'd get out on a stomach ache, head back to the rear and a bad conduct discharge and quit the Marines. I was sure that I could unjoin the Corps, since I joined. But my mind was messed up then. I wasn't thinking clearly.

Soon I heard a Lieutenant screaming for all the new guys. The sun was going down, as it was near the end of the day, and he was going to place us in our units. I don't know how, but I made it to the Lieutenant, and immediately fell flat on my back. My legs were jelly. He asked my name and placed me with 3

Charlie, which was now my squad. It was going to be a mean night, and he told us all to get to our areas and dig in. So everyone started moving away but I stayed there. The Lieutenant asked me what was wrong with me and I told him. I had a stomach ache and I needed to be choppered out. Well, needless to say that didn't go over well, especially with all the dead and wounded around us.

My stomach ache didn't rank very high. He let loose a barrage of curse words at me, yet I didn't move. I still thought he'd come to his senses and order me a chopper out of there. My plan is falling apart as I'm laying there. But that was the hope I wanted to grab on to, and that's what I did. I stayed there, as I couldn't do any more thinking. At this point, I was marked as a coward. But I was so filled with terror that I could accept that then. But I was completely exposed, both from the verbal assaults of everyone around me and the incoming fire and mortars.

I've put myself in grave danger and little chance of survival if the enemy decides to lambaste this hill. But I'm thinking about me and my exit from Vietnam. Many of the Marines around me noticed that I was no good at that point. They did their share of cursing me, hitting and kicking me and spitting on me. They called me terrible names. I was a good place to vent for these Marines who had already been through so much. But I still didn't move. I knew I'd still get through it all if I'd just make it through the night. I was stubborn, just as I was in Kindergarten; when I refused to sit in class and stood the entire semester. I don't think these Marines knew how much stubbornness I had in me. But it went on and on. It was endless, and I was breaking down. I was hopeless and frustrated. I had no peace. It was definitely the lowest point in my life.

Somewhere in the night as I was lying there, and I don't know where it came from then, I cried out as loud as I could, "God help me!" I screamed it. As soon as it came out of my mouth, I wondered what the point was. Keep in mind, I had never been to church before. We lived like Vikings, really. So church wasn't ever in my mind or plans. Why would I cry out to God? After all, I was a pagan and time was running out. Those around me seemed to think that I'd snapped. However, anyone with credentials would have called it a complete breakdown. I was in the midst of a pack of wild dogs that were having their way with me, and here comes "God Help Me"? Looking back, I see why I did it and how God was there for me that night. I didn't realize that I'd just entered into the supernatural realm as God visited me right then and there. Little did I know, that one sentence would save me time and time again throughout my tour. Words cannot describe how grateful I am. His word and his faithfulness keep me pressing towards the mark!

Here is something to take away from that moment:

When the winds of war are blowing, the wind of God knows your heart, your voice, and your cry. He will answer in a mighty way. As I lay on that warravaged mountain, it seemed all hope was lost. But something during the night rose up inside me that all hell could not stop!

Morning comes and I'm still sticking with my stomach ache story. I was still paralyzed with fear. Everyone started packing up and getting ready to leave. The officer saw I was still laying there. Orders were to move out "and leave the new guy". I thought, "They can't do that! I'm an American!" I thought they were bluffing, and I was still looking for my chopper! They started moving out in column formation off the hill. Then it clicked. There was no chopper coming. They were definitely going to leave me, and it filled me with anger. Something turned. I was mad. I couldn't believe they'd leave me out there. What would happen if the enemy found me out here? So I'm the last guy on the hill. I knew I was going to die out there, but I didn't know anything about war. At that point, I had set it in my mind that I was going to be the best. I was going to be the meanest, baddest Marine out there. I was going to find someone out there who could help me at war. The anger gave me energy. So I tossed my plan of quitting right out the window and moved out. Now I had Plan B – find someone to show me the ropes. I was a marked man, but I planned to change that very quickly.

I needed a friend then, and didn't know I already had one. His name is Jesus.

LETTERS TO HOME

April, 1968

Dear Mom & Dad & Kids,
Hi! How is everyone? Well I hope everyone had a nice Easter. I'll bet by now all the kids are sick of candy. We asked our Sergeant but he wouldn't let us have Easter baskets. I sure was disappointed...Dad, I sure do appreciate the ten dollars you sent me. I don't know what I'd do without your help. Well Dad, take it easy. Well, tomorrow I've got a big day. Our company is going on a long trip to the top of this mountain. Have you heard from Mike lately? I hope he's all right. I'll be glad when he gets home. Well I guess I better go now. I sure love and miss everyone. Love, Steve

April, 1968

Dear Mom & Dad & Kids,
How is everyone? Fine, I hope. Well, today is Tuesday, or it was. I just got back from the field. We got back early today because of bad ammunition and faulty bores in our automatic rifles. The ammunition was too old and I guess it was going off in the chamber, sometimes

exploding. One round went off or exploded, and it completely tore up a rifle. The guy was real lucky. It blew up in his face, but all it did was destroy his rifle. After that happened, a Colonel came up in the firing line and how all the automatic rifles are under survey. Then our whole company had to leave the range because of that accident...What have you been doing lately, Mom? I hope you didn't work too hard at the flower shop. Boy it sure helps when you work during the holidays. Are you still watching those kids? I'll be glad when you quit that job. You have enough to do without watching other peoples kids. Have you heard from Mike lately? You know he's only got about 80 days left. Well, I'd better go now. I love and miss all of you. Love, Steve

April, 1968

Dear Mom & Dad & Kids,

Hi! How is everyone? I sure was glad to talk to you Sunday. I forgot about dad going to a union meeting. I wanted to talk to him. Does Dad still do the cooking during supper time? Well, I had a pretty interesting day today. This morning I went to the gas chamber. I'll never forget that experience. My eyes are still swollen from the gas. Well, the first thing we did was go into the chamber with our masks on. We got in the chamber, then came the gas. After a few minutes they said take off your masks. That's when everything started happening. Some guys panicked and couldn't get their masks back on. It was funny. Some guys were so nervous they couldn't get their mask on right. They were pounding on the doors and everything. It's funny when I think about it afterwards. The main thing is to relax, but it's pretty hard to do when you're choking and you can't see. Then we had to take off our mask and sing the Marine Corps hymn. This afternoon we practiced combat tactics. Tomorrow I have to get up at three and I won't get back from the field until ten o'clock tomorrow night. It gets pretty tiring after practicing over and over. It mostly concerns different formations of the squads during combat conditions, what each man does under fire, etc. Well, I better go now. I sure love & miss all of you. Love, Steve

May, 1968

Hi! How is everyone? All right I hope! I'm sorry I didn't get to talk to you Saturday night. I couldn't call Sunday because I had guard duty. Well it's now Monday morning. It's about time now. I can't wait for May 24. I don't know what time I'll be in Indianapolis. Have you heard from Mike lately? Do you know exactly when he'll be home? I doubt if I'll be able to see him. Have you got a package with all my winter uniforms in it yet? I know you'll get this letter before Mother's Day, but I want to wish you a Happy Mother's Day! Here I'll be firing the M-16 rifle and going through tactics. I'm not sure if I'm going to try to get into recon now. We're going to a class which they'll tell us all about recon, etc. Every once in a while I see recon training platoons. They have it pretty bad. I guess you'd have to be crazy to join recon. I thought about it for a long time now. I just can't make up my mind. It's hard enough being an infantry Marine. I will write and call you on the weekends. I've only got three weekends anyway. I haven't had mail call for about five days now. I hope we'll have it tonight. I bought my plan ticket. It cost around $120.00 round trip. I think I'll just have enough money to get home and back. I won't have any money once I get home I don't think. All I want to do is get home.
Here is my schedule of my plane:
Los Angeles to Indianapolis
One stop in St Louis, Depart 4:35pm (May 24) Arrive 12 midnight.

Well Mom and Dad, I'll see you soon. I love & miss all of you. Love, Steve

June, 1968

Hi! How is everyone? Just fine I hope. Well I got to staging about ten thirty at night. I went through processing yesterday. I called you last night because I won't be able to
Sunday. I was told last night that the 1st Marine Division is relieving the 3rd Division in Saigon. I told Dad it was Da Nang. Dad I want to wish you a Happy Father's Day. I'm sorry I didn't spend much time with all of you when I was home. I really feel bad about it. Dad I decided to join the Police Department. I don't know who to see about it. Whatever you can do at home go ahead. It is what I want to do. I told you not to write me but you can before I go to Nam. Just don't write after June 28th. Please write me before I go, OK? Tell Mike I said hi. When he gets home I'll be so happy. I won't see him for over a year now. I love all of you so much. When I come home next time it will be for good. Soon as I get on the Police Department I will fix up the downstairs. Here is my address
Unit 4217
4th Replacement Co
Staging MCB Camp Pendleton
1st Marine Division 92054
Write me soon, OK? I just can't wait till I'm home again. I promise to write you as often as I can when I get to Nam. Mom, you and dad please don't worry about me. Remember, I love & miss all of you. Love, Steve

June, 1968

Hi! How is everyone? Just fine I hope. I wish I was home today. I miss all of you so much. Time is going so slow. Dad, you know when I told you I wasn't scared about going to Nam? Well don't believe that everyone here is scared. I've just got to make it back home. In thirteen months I will be back home for good. Well, tomorrow my actual training begins. I leave here next week though. Mom I'll bet you're getting a good tan. I want you and dad to relax this summer. When I start sending home money, Mom if anything comes up and you need money just take whatever I have please. And when I was home, pay Mike back for whatever I borrowed. I start making $165 a month in July. I'll be sending most of it in money orders. Well, it won't be long now till Mike's home. I can imagine how it feels. Tell him to take it easy for me. He's probably the happiest guy I the world. It's going to be a long while before I see him once again. Next July is going to be the happiest part of my life. Dad & Mom I can't tell you how much I'm going to miss you. I told you Dad that I might go to Da Nang or Phu Bai, well I'm most likely going to Saigon. Nobody really knows where we're going though. I don't feel too bad about going when I think about the thousands who went before me. I am a little scared though. Mom, you and Dad I don't want worrying about me. I'll be all right and I'll be home before you know it. Do you know, when I think of Vietnam, I want to go but then I don't. It's a good feeling knowing that you're really doing something for your country. I just don't think enough people care about this war. People don't realize how serious this war is. I do hope it ends by the time I get home. I hope you know I won't be too civilized when I get home. It will take a while to get used to living again. At least that's what I was told. When I do come back from Nam, I promise you will be proud of me. I just wish I could get over there.

This training isn't going to help me. All I think about is Nam. I just can't wait till July 5. I love & miss all of you. I'll write again real soon. Love, Steve P.S. Write me before I go over.

June, 1968

Dear Mom & Dad & Kids,
Hi! How is everyone? Just fine I hope. Well, lately all I've been doing is traveling. Last night we caught our bus to Norton Air Force Base instead of El Toro. It was about a hundred miles farther. Well, we got out at the airport about one in the morning. Then we waited till about four for our plane. We boarded the Continental plane, all 165 of us. They had beautiful stewardesses waiting for us. We ate a good meal before landing in Honolulu Hawaii. The flight took about five and a half hours. We stayed in Honolulu for about an hour. It was really beautiful. I always wanted to see Hawaii. I'll never forget that stop. Even the air in Hawaii was so different. I hope I go back some day. Well, I'm now on the same plane for Okinawa. The flight time is nine and a half hours. I'll be getting into Okinawa about ten in the morning. Somehow I lose a day. Monday, I should be stationed somewhere in Vietnam. I'll write and give you my address as soon as I know it. Dad, I never did thank you for that letter you wrote me. It made me feel good to know what a great father I have. I am looking forward to that chicken dinner… Remember, that I do love & miss all of you. Love, Steve

July, 1968

Dear Mom & Dad & Kids,
Hi! How is everyone? Just fine I hope! Well, I'm now in Okinawa. We're not leaving until next Saturday. It's like a vacation here. The

temperature and humidity is hell though. It's been pretty hard to adjust to. Your clothes are sticky from the humidity. You only have to be eighteen to drink here. I spend most of my time in this club which serves good American beer for 20 cents a can. They have a Japanese band which plays there along with tables full of dancing girls. I've been having a great time. Too bad Saturday it all has to end. I've been told I'll be stationed right around Da Nang. Today…we had to get a few more shots. I'm pretty sore right now. One shot to thin my blood. I guess that's why I feel so weak and dizzy. I still feel good enough to go to the club though. Well, I hope Mike got home by now. I sure wish I was there to meet him. Since I've been here I've lost a lot of weight. I expect to lose a lot more in Nam. Well, I miss all of you. All of you be sure to write me when you get my address. Love, Steve. P.S. Mike have a good time.

July, 1968

Dear Mom & Dad & Kids,
Hi! How is everyone? Just fine I hope! I just want to tell you that I'm fine. I've been through a little bit of hell lately, but I'm all right. After about a week on operation, they took us back to the rear to rest. The country and terrain we was fighting in was so bad we hardly had any clothes left. We were right in the DMZ. At one time I was about 100 yards from North Vietnam. I never was really serious about this war until I started seeing
things I hope I never see again. People just don't realize how terrible this war is. Since I've been on this operation, I've seen many things, especially men getting killed. I never get used to it. There are other things that make this war so hard also. A couple of our own men have been killed by our own artillery. I've seen men die from heat stroke. I'll

be so glad to just get home and forget about this war. It sure felt good to get in from the bush and get new clothes and supplies. I even took a shower last night. We did make contact with a regiment of NVA. We got word that we might be going down South tomorrow. I sure hope so. I hope you understand I can't write very often. When we go back to the rear to rest is about the only time I have to write. Please don't worry about me. I'll really be all right. I just wish I was fighting for a definite purpose. There's so much controversy about this war. Even though this war is terrible, I'm glad I'm over here doing my part. There's one thing I'll never get used to and that's killing a person. A couple of nights ago, me and six other men set up a night ambush along this creek. That's when I killed my first gook. There was only three of them. It's something I can't explain. Over here it's kill or be killed. I'll never get used to it, but it's the way it is. It won't be long till I'm home. I'd better go now. Write me soon. I do love & miss all of you. Love, Steve.

August, 1968

Dear Mike,

Hi! How have you been? Just fine I hope! I sure was glad to get your letter. Tell Mom and Dad I'm fine! I only have time for one letter, so I'm writing you because you're leaving soon. Tell Mom and Dad I'm sorry about writing, but I don't have the time right now. The last couple of days I've been up in the Dong Ha Mountains. It's close to the DMZ. I sure wish I could see your car. I always dreamed of having a Road Runner. What color is it? Mike, when you get to your next duty station, write and send me your address. Mom wanted to know what my schedule is, what I'm doing, etc. I'm going on patrols during the day. I go on listening posts at night at least five nights a week (that's really hell). Some days I go on outpost. I just search for gooks then. A few days ago I spotted gooks down in the valley and this Lieutenant let me call in the fire mission. We really messed up quite a few gooks. I called in 105 HW rounds. Well, finally tomorrow I'm leaving for Camp Carroll. I sure am glad. They've been hitting us with rockets and mortars about every night. Mike, I sure was sorry your friend Chris was killed. I know how you feel. I tell you Mike, this is a hell of a war. I've got a lot of respect for the NVA, but I love killing them. They fight a hard war. The other days we found some Marines after the gooks got through with them. I'll never forget what they did to them. It goes two ways though. I should be writing more letters when I get to Carroll. At Carroll, I'll be going on mine sweeps. The word is pretty soon our company will be going down South around Da Nang. I don't know whether I like that idea or not. There's quite a few booby traps down South and NVA. Well Mike, take care of yourself. I sure miss the family and you too. Write me soon. Love Steve.

P.S.

I sure love and miss all of you.

CRUMPLER

As I mentioned previously, at this point I am a marked man. I've been labeled as a coward on my first day. No one would speak to me, and I was looked upon with contempt. The rest of the squad saw me as someone they couldn't trust since I was of no use to them the first day I arrived in the Nam. I didn't know anything about jungle warfare, and since no one would speak to me, I was in trouble if I didn't have someone to help me through my tour.

I began reaching out to fellow squad members, and again, they'd either ignore me or curse at me. Finally after a few days of pestering people for help, someone told me I needed to talk to Crumpler, as he was the best. But they also told me that Crumpler wouldn't speak to me either, as he kept to himself most of the time.

Crumpler was a big guy, about 6'4" and 200+ pounds. I think he was a Sergeant, but I'm not sure. It was obvious he'd been in the bush a long time, because he had a reputation amongst the squad as being good at war. He was a bad dude. But like the men said, he kept quiet and stayed alone. He never talked about himself to anyone. Crumpler was always a guy who was cool under pressure. He always kept his composure under any circumstance, and his kill zone was a wide one. Being new to the jungle, when we engaged in a firefight, in the beginning my reaction was to hit the deck. He never did. Matter of fact, we got into a firefight once, and he actually shot an NVA in the chest with a bloop gun. Talk about something right out of the movies! We were all impressed. He showed no emotion. To Crumpler, it was just another day at the office. He was on another planet. He was a machine, always prepping for war. Looking back, he also never answered to anyone. Ever.

I pestered Crumpler for a couple of days and yep, he ignored me. He'd tell me to go away or leave him alone, and it discouraged me. I'd ask for help and he'd tell me to go get him some coffee. I'd do that and he'd tell me to hit the road. But I didn't give up. I needed to learn and no one would teach me. Finally, after my relentless pestering, he told me to sit down and listen.

I have to say, Crumpler taught me more than I could imagine and more than I learned in boot camp and AIT. He gave me details on things. Details I needed. He took the time to teach me about maps and compasses. He taught me how to break down my weapons and clean them so they would not jam. He taught me about trip wires, how to set up my perimeter, kill zone strategies and working the clock. He taught me about L ambushes and how the NVA liked to use that technique. In an

L ambush, they'd let the point go through and collapse the L on the column. They'd attack the rear a lot of times instead of going through the point. These things I did not know when I arrived.

He mentioned things that they didn't teach you in boot camp, like how the NVA would set up booby traps. The NVA liked to booby trap dead bodies. Sometimes, they'd leave their own in the bush and set a trap on it. So you never wanted to touch any of the dead bodies that had been there a while. Chances were it was booby trapped. The NVA was good at setting up booby traps, and Crumpler briefed me on just about all of them.

He also taught me how to smell the enemy. Due to their diet, the NVA just smelled different. Couple that with the intense heat all the time and you have fishy sweat, and that's just what they smelled like. At times, you could even smell their breath. You see sometimes on Hollywood movies, the protagonist being able to "smell" the enemy coming. Well, that's not Hollywood in the jungle. You could actually smell them. Crumpler was very good about smelling them, and he taught me how to as well. He reminded me to look at things that were changed in the jungle – things that stood out as abnormal. If the terrain changed, there was probably something there. He was good at looking for where they'd killed the jungle down in spots, whether they were for punji pits or spider holes.

I'd say one of the most important things he taught me was how to walk the point and to listen. Being new in the bush, the new guys always got stuck running point. So we lost a lot of new guys. I knew I was going to be running point soon, and thanks to Crumpler, I was prepared. Walking point was definitely scary. Not only did you have to be on high alert for enemy soldiers, but the booby traps and trip wires would get you if you weren't paying attention. Listening was important. You always had to listen - to hear the snap of a twig or movement of any kind. Each step had to be slow and deliberate, as the NVA was very sneaky when they set up booby traps, and even sneakier when they hid out quietly. So your body was always tense. There was never anyone in a hurry, so thank God when I was on point, I could move as slowly as I wanted. The point's job was to keep everyone behind him alive.

I truly owe my survival in Vietnam to Crumpler. Without his help and teaching, I surely wouldn't have made it long. I'm eternally grateful to him for teaching me about jungle warfare. Crumpler was good at war, and he in turn made me good too. I'm not sure if he was CIA. He very well could have been. I spent three months with Crumpler and then he was gone. I've not seen him since. Knowing him, I'm sure he got out alive. Where he is now, I do not know. But wherever he is and if he's reading this, I want him to know that I thank him for taking me under his wing and making me good at war.

LEARNING THE JUNGLE

One of the things that never made sense to me in Vietnam was how all of the new guys were always put on point. That strategy isn't smart, since we never knew what we were doing or looking for. What Crumpler poured into me definitely helped throughout my tour. Short timers didn't want to do point, so I ended up on it often. The learning curve was sharp, because if you weren't on your game, we were all dead, since the enemy loved taking out the point. This is why you had to read the jungle. You always had to know where the machine gun nests were, the trip wires and the snipers. There's so much to take in, and you have to take it in quickly. If you didn't, you could lose a leg, an eye or even your life. In a jungle, there's a lot to look at and a lot you won't see, which is different than what they're dealing with in Iraq.

Try moving around in a thick forest that you've never seen and you'll understand quickly. So you have to dial into it and be in tune. After a short while, your senses and hearing get very keen. Your eyesight becomes better and your five senses go to new levels. That's because your life and the lives of the others depend upon it. You pick up on it quickly or you die.

The bottom line with Crumpler was that he gave me the edge I needed. The wealth of data and information is hard to measure. He was so valuable at the time. He covered so much ground for me in such a short time. I am in great gratitude to him for taking time to teach me when I was a marked man entering the war.

We didn't get to go back to the rear often. They put us on mission after mission and firefight after firefight. We operated deep in the bush, both in Laos and Cambodia. We went where the enemy was. We knew early on that if we were killed, it was covered. We knew we weren't supposed to be there. There were a lot of covert ops and we were part of quite a bit of it. The politicians were playing games and so was everyone else. The CIA was working with them directly, and they provided supplies and other necessities during the war. It was all a game and everyone in control was lying. We were right in the midst of it. The media did a good job of covering the game and providing mistaken info to the people back in the United States. The only news we got was the jungle news.

So I'm starting to really tune in and get good at understanding this jungle war. My first day was in the past and I was well into Plan B. Through going out on patrol and working the point, I quickly got very good at war. I'd come a long way from my first day, and was really transformed. Perhaps I was too dialed in, I don't know. I was just motivated to learn so I could live and go to college. I got really good. I got really good at being a killer. Quickly I got dialed into the war and became consumed with it.

My senses were heightened and all my concentration was on staying alive at all costs.

Very quickly I was transformed into someone I had never been. I went a complete 180 from being the coward on the first day to kill kill kill. I became an animal. Now I'm entrenched in this thing called war. I'm good as far as I'm concerned. I've adjusted and adapted, but unfortunately, it was in the other direction.

One time, we were set up on a hill where the enemy was sending wave after human wave at us. Their job was to overrun the line and break through the perimeter. Once they did that, the "good" NVA soldiers could come through and kill us. So the human waves were sacrifices. They would strap bombs on themselves and attempt to get through the line. They would send old people, women, children, you name it. It's a lot of trigger time, put it that way. The next day, the order was to clean up your kill zone, which meant eliminating the wounded, taking their weapons and stacking the bodies. You still have to be on high alert, since the waves may have satchel charges that they haven't lit. So you had to be careful.

So you drag the bodies to a part of the hill and stack them. You do the same with the weapons. Once that was done, some of the Marines had cameras and wanted to take pictures. I decided to eat my lunch on top of the dead bodies. What was going through my head at the time, I do not know. But I was dialed into the war. Again, perhaps I was too dialed in. I grabbed a couple of their heads under my arms and they took my picture. I posed for several shots. I actually took that film and sent that home to my parents to have them develop them. That should explain how "gone" I was. I didn't think at the time that they'd shock my parents and brothers and sisters. I just thought they'd be cool pictures. A Captain came out of the bunker in the center of the hill and saw us all on top of the dead bodies. The look on his face was blank. He was almost cringing, knowing we'd certainly snapped; and we had.

Another time, I remember I was coming into a group of Marines that I had never worked with. They had just been through some real hell and under siege. They had trouble with a Second Lieutenant who had the day before got a bunch of Marines killed. Apparently the enemy had hit them with a .30 cal and he'd ordered them to go online and take it out. He was probably new to jungle war and his tactics were way off. I'd seen this before, as many of the officers they'd sent over weren't that good.

I dropped my pack, as I'd been humping all day and sat down. I was observing a small group of Marines nearby who had formed a circle. These guys were drawing straws. These straws were for who was going to kill that Second Lieutenant that night. I was in disbelief. I didn't think they'd do something like that, so I was in awe. So not long after, I asked them what they were planning on doing and they advised me to keep an ear to the radio that night, as they were going to take out the Second Louie. I still didn't believe it.

As planned later that night, they were called out on a patrol and sure enough, the Second Lieutenant was going with them. We listened on the radio about an hour and a half after they left and there was a lot of chatter. Suddenly the chatter on the radio was that the Second Lieutenant had been hit and they were bringing him in. That was my first encounter with a situation like that, and believe it or not, that happened often. It never had a right feel to me, and I'm glad, but I also understand it somewhat, as there were so many orders that just didn't make sense and got a lot of men killed.

All that being said, you have to reach deep when it comes to war. We are fighting every day. Our life is at stake every minute. The enemy is around every turn. You don't know if it's your time that day or you live until tomorrow. So it messes with your psyche at every moment. The only thing you're really thinking about is how you can stay alive. For me, that meant stacking as many bodies as I could. If I got them first, they didn't get me. There are no niceties. Throw that right out the window. Whoever you were back in the States, forget it. You are someone else now. You have to be someone else. None of that means anything. The only thing that matters now is your world here. If hell could be described, that was it. There was no way out except in a body bag, you're wounded or you do your twelve and twenty. The laws of the jungle are very simple – it's kill or be killed. That's what you have got to apply every day in the jungle. It's very simple and very final. You're not troubled with the meaningless drama back home. It's a weird parallel, but that's just the way it is.

MONSOON RAINS AND THE JUNGLE SOLDIER'S THINKING

I found myself on a mission with a small unit up in North Vietnam. The mission was to capture as many prisoners and documents as we could. It was a covert mission in the Dong Ha Mountains. We had maybe two or three squads. The only thing different about this mission were the monsoon rains, which no one had briefed us on. When it rains, it rains for days and it's a constant downpour. Up in the mountains, it gets cold too. Couple that with a very thick canopy and you have a recipe for Mother Nature's wrath.

We had captured some NVA and some documents, so that part of the mission was successful. Then it began to rain. It continued to rain and didn't stop. Monsoon had started. Visibility was terrible. You couldn't even start a fire or make a cup of coffee. We soon got word that we wouldn't be extracted as planned, as no choppers could fly in the rains. The rations we took were nearly exhausted, as this was supposed to be a very short mission. If the enemy was going to hit us, this would have been a good time, since we couldn't see or hear anything. At night, it was freezing cold. Nothing was dry to keep you warm. I simply put a poncho liner over my head and kept blowing on my hands to keep them warm.

This went on day after day and the choppers still couldn't come get us. But we didn't know to expect this. Apparently, they didn't need us to know this was coming. Believe it or not, the rain was driving us all crazy, as if we weren't crazy already! So here we were watching these NVA soldiers whom we had blindfolded and tied to trees, and the pounding rain, lack of sleep and lack of food just drove us over the edge. We decided to do something to keep us occupied. We decided to play a game. A very sick game. We decided that our game was that each of us would get to line up and hit the prisoners one time. You couldn't hit them twice or kick or stab them. You just got one hit.

I was in line and by the time I got to them, they were already slumped over and most likely dead. The men in front of me were punching these prisoners as hard as they could in the head and temple, so it was only a matter of time. Not much of a game, really. Eventually we just killed them all, because we were losing it. After five or six days of no food, no rest and the constant rain, we just lost control. It was an unbelievable setting we were in, and time was passing so slowly. There was nothing to hear but the pounding of the rain.

We were out there for eleven days.

On the eleventh day, I'm not even sure my weapon will fire. I had been suffering from what they called "Immersion Hands". I had open cracks and cuts to where I could hardly close my hands or use them. Had I had to pull the trigger, it would have been so painful. But I wasn't even sure if I did pull the trigger that it would even fire. Many of us were even hallucinating. The dead prisoners were rotting and smelling by now and we were freezing.

There was then a break in the rain and they finally got a chopper to us and extracted us. We were choppered to a rear area base and the first thing I wanted was a hot cup of coffee and shower. My feet had immersion injuries as well. We were all pretty messed up. I had never experienced this and never want to again. Monsoon season was well in hand now, and I knew all I ever wanted to know about it. It's just one of the many types of hell that was thrown at us. We spent two or three days in the rear after that. It happened so quickly. We longed for the day we got back to the rear to get some hot chow, beer and rest. But again, the thinking of the soldier out there in the jungle is twisted. Even after spending eleven days in hell, after just a couple days in the rear, we wanted back out there. There's really no explanation for the schizophrenic type thinking of the jungle soldier. It doesn't make sense, but that's what we were thinking. What's the next mission? It's insanity all the way. The bush was our home. One particular operation we were out for 110 days straight without a shower.

During monsoon season, choppers don't fly. So there were different tactical ideas that needed to be implemented, both on missions and supply chains. They couldn't send us as far out as they would have liked since the extraction points would be hard to get to in the monsoon. This goes the same for getting weapons and supplies in and out of the fire base, as well as getting the dead and wounded out. It limited our capabilities as to our usual operations.

So some idiot came up with the "Pacification" program. The thinking behind it was because it was monsoon season, let's take the troops we had and send them into the villages to win the hearts and minds of the local people. Our job was to take our unit and squad to a village with 100 ARVN troops, update their weaponry and train them on weapons and tactics. Their weaponry was outdated as well, so we replaced them. I had an ARVN colonel who reported to me in the village inside Quang Tri Province. We had to teach them on ambushes, how to use Laws rockets, grenades, you name it. Little did we know, we were in heavy VC country, and the very ARVN troops we were assigned to train and pacify were actually The VC!

The VC's supply line actually ran directly through the village we were in. The villagers were relatives and friends of the VC, which we didn't know at the time. They'd feed and update the VC as they passed through the area. Knowing the area as we did not, they hung around the outskirts of the village, out of our sites. I'll discuss the Pacification program and our adventures in the village in another chapter.

SANDBAGGING

Anyone who's been to Vietnam knows about sandbagging. From time to time, depending on who's in charge, you get these insane orders that just never make sense. This is Charlie's country and sandbagging comes from too many of those crazy orders coming down from the top. We'd often get sent out in small groups, often outnumbered, and we were always in dangerous territory. The conditions were tiring, so there had to be some shortcuts. So we'd take the orders that were given and cut them down to our perspective and to what we thought would be best. We had to look out for ourselves since no one was looking out for us. But it had to be unanimous. We all had to agree to sandbag. But I don't remember anyone ever protesting!

So we'd get our orders from the top to go out on a patrol. Maybe there would be several checkpoints along the way and we'd be out for the whole day. So we'd hump for a while (and this would often get very tiring) and eventually cut corners to make the mission shorter. We'd set up a bit rather than being stretched out against incredible odds and stay pat. We'd get our orders, sit down as a group and discuss the mission and then decide if we were going to sandbag. Many times, I'd take the coordinates and cut them in half, which saved us a lot of time, and so on and so on. We'd eventually end up at the end of the mission, but it cut our time in half. They knew everyone did it. They just rarely caught anyone.

But the point of the mission is to make contact. They want you to encounter the enemy. So if we ran into any resistance or enemy presence, we had our radio and could call in 155s or 175s from the firebase and drop artillery on the area. With all we went through in the bush, we didn't always want to come in contact with the enemy. But if we did, we had assets at our disposal.

On this particular mission, we were in Laos on a covert operation. The territory was brutal. It was like the Amazon, very ridgy with deep waterfalls. It was brutal but beautiful. We eventually ran across a prime spot to set up, which was across from a waterfall. Not only was it a place where we could relax and have a much welcome swim, but it had a high point at the top of the waterfall which gave us a great view of the surrounding area. It was lush, something you'd see in a vacation magazine. Beautiful green trees, clear, calm water – just an amazing place. So clearly we were all ecstatic and in great need of a little bit of R&R, as we normally wouldn't find spots like this to sandbag.

We quickly set up our perimeter and our security area high on the ridge and prepared for a day of relaxation. I was in command, and I allowed only a few guys to swim at a time, maybe an hour or so and then we'd switch off. We knew we had plenty of time, since the missions lasted the entire day. So everyone would have their opportunity to get in the water. So I called the firebase on the radio and informed them that we'd passed our checkpoint and moving towards the next. Let the sandbagging begin!

We were really enjoying our time in that area, and taking advantage of the beautiful surroundings to kick back and enjoy ourselves. However, because of the waterfall noise, we didn't hear the spotter plane flying over us! They sent spotter planes all the time, and they were very quiet. Their job was to fly over and check for movement along different areas. They have no weapons, so they wait to see movement, and then

they call in artillery.

I get a call from command, "Three Charlie, this is Hotel. Please relay your coordinates again." I told them we're past Checkpoint A and onto Checkpoint B, which was bogus of course. Apparently the spotter plane saw one of my men jump from the top of the waterfall into the water below, so there was the movement he'd been looking to spot. Command just wanted to confirm the movement and see if there were any friendlies in the area. So I replied back to them that there were none (without checking our grid) and that again, we were past Checkpoint A and well on our way to

Checkpoint B. After that, I thought nothing of it.

Fifteen minutes later, wouldn't you know it, artillery starts to drop on us into our position. I get back on the radio and call the firebase, "Hotel be advised we're taking enemy fire!" They asked me what our position was and with our cover blown, I just admitted it. "Hotel, we're sandbagging! Call off the fire mission now!" I had no choice! If we didn't, they'd have fired for effect and we'd have been toast.

Command comes back over the radio, "Get back here Mitchell! You're gonna be court-martialed!" I know I'm in deep deep trouble at this point. I was going to end up in the brig and they were going to throw away the key. We make our way back to the firebase, where they took my command away from me. Who should I run into again? The Sergeant (who I'll talk about later), who was happy to tell me that when I got back to the rear I was going to get court-martialed.

Luckily, and by God's grace again nothing ever came of it. Once again, God came through and showed himself by not only saving my life and the lives of my men, but keeping me out of the brig.

PACIFICATION

Pacification was one of the strangest parts of my tour of duty in Southeast Asia. I was briefed on the fly, and it wasn't well thought out. Had someone taken the time to plan this thing out, I promise you they would have never, ever used us for a mission like this. It was a recipe for disaster, and sure enough, disaster came real quick in this village. Looking back though, I am reminded of a scripture in Ephesians 6:12

"For we wrestle not against flesh and blood, but against principalities, against powers, against the rulers of the darkness of this world, against spiritual wickedness in high places."

Since this is a story with military missions and strategies, I'm going to walk you through this by the numbers in order to expose valuable data left out of the equation. We've all heard it said that information is on a need to know basis. I thought it would be best to let you decide.

Vietnam was a country that was ripe for a smorgasbord of evil. The hostile atmosphere attracted every demon that could be assigned, because there was plenty of overtime. In a war, there must be planning, and from the planning stage objectives are born. The planning here was done by a group that had to include some drunken sailors. One clear objective here was to win the hearts and minds of the people. Lessons learned here are that it's critical that you know what you're up against, and this includes troop strength, terrain, air force and all military hardware from tanks to guns. It's also important to first try and understand their religious and political beliefs. It's obvious that our government did not do their due diligence, for if they had, they would have come to a logical conclusion to abort and scrap the whole idea. I was limited in my knowledge of Buddhism. My impression of a Buddhist monk was someone who was peaceful, tranquil and one who meditated all day. That idea had holes all over the place.

Buddhism has been a stronghold for centuries. China introduced Confucianism through a monk named Mou Po. He was the first major apostle in Vietnam. Cambodia and Japan added their influences, and they ended up with about sixteen different varieties of Buddhism. Now add to that the war, infighting, dissension and divisions and you've got a wicked mix of devils running wild, attaching themselves to anyone or anything that entertained the dark side. This also included séances and chanting (which included curses) and ancestor and animal worship throughout the whole land. When I walked through the jungles of Vietnam, one of the strongest memories I have is that of a constant presence of evil. Now at the time, my spiritual discernment was nonexistent. However, since I was the target of this Eastern cult religion, I can speak from firsthand experience. The Buddhists were Viet Cong allies. That put a weird spin on things. But truth be told, the country of Vietnam was filled with religious fanatics that would never give peace of democracy a chance. Obviously, my idea of a Buddhist monk was way off base!

They were extremists to their cause. The level of commitment could be seen throughout the world when a monk doused himself with gasoline and set himself on fire. He was committed. Someone should have been watching this. We are now replaying the same story in a different place. Muslim extremists are committed to sacrifice themselves to prove their point to the infidels. These followers of false Gods believe they are on a swift journey to the next life in paradise, and they kill as many others as possible. From Vietnam to Iraq to Afghanistan, the war planners have grossly underestimated the spiritual strongholds and their committed belief system. In Vietnam, they fired their own children up with heroin, put explosive backpacks on them and sent them into our midst to kill us. Islam, Buddhism and more are an extreme brand of believers of the most twisted and radical beliefs in the world today – and yet they call themselves peaceful. History has shown us the results, but we seem unable to learn this lesson.

So as the truck stops and we're unloading on our first day in Quang Tri, I see another squad being dropped off further up the road. That was the plan, as several squads were dropped off throughout the Quang Tri region. Several squads were spaced out in the region, each with their own villages and missions. It was a dirt road entering the village, with grass roofed huts and hooches. Nothing was fancy. Ouside the hooches was a black pot for cooking rice and rat. It was a very simple life for them. I imagine it may cost you $27 to build something like that. The people were very poor. The only thing that mattered to them it seemed was how were they going to feed themselves every day?

I would assume there were between two to three hundred people in the village. Down the way was a river, where they fished, bathed, washed their clothes and got their water for cooking and drinking. They'd take their bamboo poles and buckets and get their water for the day. Surrounding the village was a vast setting of rice paddies.

Outside of the rice paddies was a grazing area where herds of water bull would graze. They were used for heavy work and carrying things from village to village. Near there stood pagoda temples, where they would burn incense and worship Buddha.

My first job was to set a perimeter around the village and set a security detail. Rather than set up slowly and calmly and establish good relations with the people, my very curious men decided to take it South very quickly. They began mingling through the village under the guise of recon, but were actually looking to make their mark on the villagers. One of my men actually picked up a small child, threw him into the air and broke his arm. The people started screaming and yelling. So I approached him and placed my M16 under his chin and explained to him that we didn't do that here. That was the last thing I needed was my men acting up. So we had a little standoff there. So it was already going crazy, and we had just gotten there.

We should have never been assigned this mission. My men and I were trained killers at this point. Our tempers were short-fused, we had hair triggers and no patience. Anyone and anything that looked VC, we killed. Even though our orders in the past were to obtain and retrieve prisoners, we never let them live. We came across a team of dead Marines in the bush who were tortured and chopped up. From that point on, we never let any prisoner live. So we were not in any shape or form to pacify anyone at this point, as we'd been out in the bush so long. No one at the top thought that through. We were never prepared for this mission. We didn't care about these people and didn't want to be there. Dealing with these people was going to be a bad thing. It was falling apart from Jump Street.

My men were already out of control, and I wasn't set up to control these problems. Any problems I had in the past were dealt with by me simply killing the enemy. But this was a different animal, and there was no way that any of us should have been there, unless you wanted the village wiped out. I wish I could say that things settled down in the village, but they were always heating up. It was one fire after another. There was no way to do any damage control when you have several problems going on at once - one of which started not long after we began training the ARVN troops.

The first thing on my mind was to get to training them. We needed a change of pace. I didn't want to leave a pile of Laws rockets lying around. I knew the VC were close, but never knew what to expect on their attacks or how they would do it. I wasn't used to setting up in a village setting with civilians. From what I could see from the ARVNs, they were useless and of no help. They weren't good at war. None of them had a look of anything except a look of goofiness.

I looked across the river and saw all the pagoda temples. They were about 10-12 feet high, made out of cement with a roof and an altar for them to burn incense. At the time, I had no idea that these were their churches or places of worship. To them, they were sacred. I didn't know about their religions or Buddha. I just saw the temples as great targets for training them on how to use the rockets. Think of the Laws rocket as a mini bazooka. It was a hand held anti-tank propelled grenade that caused great destruction. I ordered my men to gather as many of the rockets and head to the river with the ARVNs.

I told the ARVNs to sit down and we'd begin training on how to use the rockets. My men were briefing them on how to break down the rocket and get it ready to launch. So I pick one up and have a target set in my sights - one of their temples. I press the plunger and blow the temple up, which was about 100 yards away. The villagers start going crazy, wailing and screaming. My men love the explosion. We look to see many of the other villagers running to our location. The place is chaos now and I'm ordering my men to shut them up. The ARVNs are protesting, and again, we don't know what's going on. But my men now have them at gunpoint. One of my other men blew up another temple, and then another one. The villagers are now chanting at us. At the time I didn't know, but they were putting curses on us. We didn't understand the value they placed on the temples. We didn't know how valuable these temples were to them and their religion. We eventually used all the Laws rockets and blew up nearly every one of their temples. Of course, the ARVNs refused to fire on them.

That was the end of Laws rocket training.

I really didn't know the depth of damage we caused them that day. One of their daily outlets in their life of squalor was going to church. It was very important to them, and we destroyed it. I didn't know it then, but after that my men and I were marked. Conversation, communication and relations were out the window now. The ARVN Colonel highly protested, so I had to get in his face. So we're not off to a good start either. The village was in a real mess now. He contacted my command and next thing I know I'm being yelled at by a Second Lieutenant, who then informed me about the buildings being their churches. I told him I wasn't briefed on that, and that I didn't know. It got heated between me and the Lieutenant and I was threatened with court martial. So I complied, and that was the end of that.

Since it is still monsoon season, we're not getting much in the way of supplies into the village. One of the things we used to do was fish with hand grenades in the river. We'd bring the fish to mama san and she'd cook them up in the pot with rice for us. It was a nice change of pace from the C rations. They would also cook up rice whiskey which, the best way I could describe it would be Vietnamese moonshine. This stuff was almost pure alcohol, and would clearly do the job very quickly.

Payback came to me in the way of some poisoned rice whiskey. I had already been marked as a cursed man by them for blowing up their temples. Since we always got drunk on the rice whiskey, it was an easy way to get to us. One day, mama san handed me a bottle specifically for me. Of course I drank it down. The next day, I woke up and was totally blind. I had no sight whatsoever. Immediately I thought maybe I got a hold of a bad batch. But then I realized that mama san had poisoned me. But as I mentioned earlier about how I had already been given the edge by the Lord, I had it then. This poison was not going to kill me. I was blind yes, but not going to die.

So for three days, I could not see. My friend Junior and some of the other guys had to lead me around. We kept it quiet among everyone else. No one said anything to anyone, and I thought at the time I was done. I just didn't know what to do. Those three days of blindness were very bleak for me. I didn't know if it was to be permanent or what. I spent three days in the hooch. The Second Lieutenant decided he was going to arrive in our village to check things out. Great. How was I going to deal with that? He showed up and he knew something was wrong with me, of course. He didn't know I was blind as like I said, we kept it quiet. He just assumed I had drunk too much. Thanks to the Lord, I dodged that bullet, and on the fourth day I got my sight back. As you can see, things aren't going as planned in Quang Tri Village.

One of the things we were briefed on in the village was the many things that could kill you besides the enemy. One of those things was the bamboo viper. It was a relatively small snake that grew between 2 and 3 feet long. It was a very quiet, nocturnal snake, but very aggressive. Its bite could kill you very quickly. We were always taught to beware of the bamboo viper. That was the one snake you didn't want to see. They often called the snake the "one step". If it bites you, after one step you're dead. So if you saw one, you either killed it or got away from it. So what were the chances that a bamboo viper and I would come into close contact? In Quang Tri village I found that all things are possible.

I was lying in a hooch one morning just waking up to start my day. As I'm waking up, who could appear laying on my chest but the one thing I didn't want to meet? The bamboo viper. If I twitch and it bites me, I'm done. I'm frozen stiff with fear. There wasn't anything I could do. It seemed like time went on forever, knowing there's a snake on my chest that could kill me. But as luck would have it, (I don't want to call it luck, I had the edge), he eventually lost interest in me and crawled away back into the jungle. That was definitely one of the more frightening moments in Quang Tri. It seemed like I had these moments often in this particular village.

So we continued to go through the motions in the village. We went on several night missions as we trained them on maps, M16s and M1 carbines. All seemed to be going relatively well. We were anxious again to get out of there, but due to the monsoon rains, we were still stuck there for the time being. It's still a very dark and eerie place. At the time I didn't know, but the demonic forces were well at work there. It was very creepy.

I was coming up to a hooch one afternoon and I heard the mama san screaming inside. It sounded like she was in a fight. I enter the hooch and see a rat. She's trying to stun it with her broom, and I tell her "Lai Dai" (come here) so I can shoot it with my M16. She didn't want me to do that. So she stunned it, took it outside and hung it upside down on a string. She cut the rat's throat and let it bleed out. It's a very strange thing to witness. Well, that happened to be tonight's dinner, which was why she didn't want me to blow it up. So she cooked us up some rat and rice since we had to save our grenades and we had no way to get fish. Our C rations were about gone, so it was rat for supper. That never set well with me. At that point, I would eat just about anything, but I don't recommend rat.

One night, after days and days of eating rat and rice I'd had enough of it. I took an M1 carbine from an ARVN and informed my men I was going out to get a bird for us all. Now we're in heavy VC country, and it wasn't very smart to go out alone hunting for a bird. But my mind wasn't right at the time. I was sick of everything and all I thought about was putting something different in that pot that night. So I leave the village and the first thing I do is come to the grazing area with all the water bull. These are 1,000 pound animals, but very docile and tame animals. They're intimidating, but very domesticated. They happen to also be a very sacred animal to the people there. But I wasn't armed with that information. I'm walking directly through the herd towards my bird hunt, and I instinctively slapped one on the rear end. I kept walking and out of my peripheral, I catch movement. It was a water bull, but I'm not too concerned about it.

I kept walking and I noticed that it had a bead on me and walking in my direction. I sped up a bit and it did too. I start to get nervous. I speed up again and it speeds up again. By this time, I'm out of the grazing area and off on a dead run. The water bull is running towards me as well. I notice then I have a serious problem here. I run down an incline and the bull is right behind me, all contorted. Its horns are down and it's dead on me. Now I'm running for my life. My finger is on the trigger now. I turn around and I'm unloading this 40 round clip on my M1 carbine into this bull. I'm thinking to myself, "I'm going to die by a water bull, after all I've been through and the many times I've faced death? This is how I'm going to die?" I hit the bottom of the incline and ran into a tree. My back is against the tree and I'm screaming and shooting every bullet in this clip. The bull, snorting and contorted, came to a halt and died at my feet. This thing would have gored me if not for the edge – which showed itself yet again.

This was part of the curse and demonic activity in the village. The bull was clearly demon possessed. It was all contorted and was one of the strangest things I've seen. My adrenaline is off the charts, sitting there thinking about what had just happened. My men showed up, running towards me thinking that maybe I'd come across some VC. When the villagers saw that I'd killed a water bull, they went insane. I had not only destroyed their temples, but now I'd killed one of their sacred bulls. Now here come the chants and screams, the hysterical crying and further curses. They want me dead now. Strike two. I am really a marked man now. I am their worst enemy. Of course, my men are ecstatic, thinking they're going to eat steak tonight.

Then comes the chatter on the radio from command screaming, "Mitchell, what are you thinking!?! These are sacred animals to these people. What is going on with you?" I tried to explain what happened, that I was trying to hunt for a bird and that the water bull tried to kill me. But they're not buying it at all. Perhaps they were thinking I was drunk or high, but they do just not believe me. So another threat of court martial is thrown at me. That thing, for whatever reason was trying to kill me. That's that. I can't explain it. I know they're docile. I know they don't attack like that, but this one did and it tried to kill me!

Looking back, the spiritual connotation is clear. It wasn't really the bullets that killed that bull, it was the edge that had been given to me the day I screamed "God help me!" on my first day in Nam. Yes, I had put rounds in it, but the edge was there. Just the momentum of this 1,000 bull running at full speed alone would have killed me. But I believe an angel stopped the bull at my feet by whatever means necessary. It was my edge. It was THE edge.

But from then on, it went from bad to worse in this village. After blowing up their temples and killing a sacred bull, can you imagine what list of theirs I was on now? You can only imagine after I've insulted their religion. The last thing you would want in a village like that is them wanting you dead. It would be the equivalent of blowing up a mosque in Iraq and THEN drawing a picture of Mohammed – all the while living in a city in Iraq. To say I was a dead man was putting it mildly. Satan had tried to take me out, but he'd failed. They had marked me for death, but God had already marked me for life! He honored my cry on that lonely hill that first day. He showed up time and time again. It was not because of anything I deserved, but it was because of God's grace and faithfulness to me. His "edge" always showed up at the right time to deliver me.

QUANG TRI

I keep reemphasizing that this series in the chain of events in his village were beyond comparison as far as my tour there. Based on the scenarios that played out in this village, it was amazing that any of us made it out alive. The whole time was a bust.

Early one morning as we awaken from a drunken stupor from the night before and yes I didn't learn much of a lesson from the poison rice whiskey. I just chalked it up to a bad batch. But for release, this rice was the pretty potent and got you drunk real quick. So we continued to hit the hooch as often as we could. As we slowly woke up with a rather severe hangover, it was an eerie feeling. As you collect yourself and then wake up, I found that apparently the watch that was supposed to happen the night before never happened. My men fell asleep after drinking too much. Due to a combination of events at the time, we were becoming very careless and this was one of those times. But that wasn't like us.

Because when you let your guard down, you pay a price.

As I'm coming out of the hooch, I noticed that there was no one in the village. My men started collecting themselves and we met together in the center of the village where we all notice that everyone was gone. It was like everyone had disappeared, like out of a science-fiction movie or something. It was a very eerie feeling like "what happened?" We're obviously concerned, since the ARVNs were gone too. By now we've all got our weapons and are ready for anything because this was something very wrong in this village

So we tried to cover as much ground as we could. We made our way to river and saw no movement. Not a peep. Now we're starting to get really concerned, because we just lost a whole village!

So we moved off into a grazing area where the water bulls gathered. It was a pretty good sized open area, and we see smoke going up in the air. Some campfires are going. There are about 17 of us now that are spread out and we're about 300 yards away. As we move online with still blurred vision, our adrenaline is kicking in. As we get closer we can see some villagers. In the crowd, you can start to make out some VC, as we could see the AKs from a distance. We saw that the VCs had the villagers lined up and now we're wondering what to do in a situation like that. We're thinking anything can happen.

So with an obviously unclear head, I give the order to kill them all - just wipe them all out. That's all I can come up with at the time. I'm thinking, hey we have to kill the VC, these villagers are not my friends anyway and we have to do something. What could I say? A firefight and they got in the way? So we start firing into the crowd. Clip after clip. It was surreal. It was almost the same situation as the napalm bomb (which I'll talk about later), as I'm waiting for my men to turn to me and say, "Mitch are you seeing this? Nobody's hitting the ground, how can we miss?" Keep in mind, we were all expert marksmen. But no one was saying anything. It was like my men and I had entered a different zone. We're all still moving forward and I can hear the M16s firing, and not one person is hitting the ground. I can't explain it; it was as though I was in some supernatural zone (which I had never considered).

So we're firing and moving forward and the VC eventually made it through the other side of the crowd and they got away. We made it to the crowd and not one civilian had taken a hit. It was the miracle of all miracles that you could imagine in this natural realm. My men beat up a few of the people, as we let our anger get the best of us and they were feeding the VC, which they had been forced to do. Several of the people were beat up, and we just dropped it. Looking back, the ARVNs leaving was just another issue of them actually being VC, which we didn't know at the time.

We needed to get out of this village very soon. Problem was, it came from the top and you can't push Mother Nature. When it's clear when the monsoons are over, perhaps we'd be able to get outta Dodge, which would be a good day. But this was the layer effect in this village, with the curses and spiritual end of things. It was of a very dark village very eerie because of the demonic curses and the demonic activity that was released there daily. It didn't help that we blew up their temples and killed their water bull. There were many agendas going on at the same time. I'm sure if they could have had the chance to kill us in our sleep, they would have. Perhaps that's why they gave us the rice wine that night. But in a war situation in VC territory, you don't let your guard down.

THE NIGHT AMBUSH

Tensions were already high in Quang Tri village. We had blown up their pagoda temples, killed a sacred water bull and been poisoned with rice wine. We hadn't been there but maybe two weeks, and it is already chaos. With all that already happening, I'd never imagined something even crazier was about to occur.

Continuing our orders for Pacification, we had already attempted to train the ARVN troops on map reading, weapons and tactics and jungle warfare. They didn't seem interested in learning any of it. But we pressed on. The next step was to train them on night patrols, listening posts and ambush setups.

Earlier in the day, I went out alone to scout the area. I went a few clicks from the village and found a nice spot along a tree line which sat along a river. It looked like a great spot for the VC to cross over into the village, so I set my area up to prepare for a night ambush. It was the perfect spot. So I went back into the village to set up my squad.

I chose three of my men and three of the ARVNs to come along on the night ambush. We brought plenty of weapons and a BAR, which I loved. Although it was a World War 2 weapon, it still packed a punch. So the ARVN accompanying me was in charge of that weapon. We got on line a bit before dark and waited for the enemy to show up. That is what many of those night patrols were like – a waiting game. They're normally very boring. But I was certain we'd have contact that night. Before hand, I briefed the ARVNs not to do anything until they were given the green light from me. As soon as you see me give the OK, light up the tree line.

It was about 11 o'clock and all was quiet. It was also a full moon, so you knew something crazy was about to take place. We started hearing noises, and I knew they were coming. I specifically heard a squishy sound as they moved out of the tree line into the wet mud at the bank of the river. As they moved closer to us, due to the full moon we could make out silhouettes of seven VC.

The plan was to allow the seven to cross the river. Once they crossed over, they'd attempt to secure the tree line, and then they would send the rest who were surely following behind them. Of course, we're jacked. Adrenaline was high to say the least. I remember they had something they were floating on as they passed through the river to our side. After a few moments, the seven made it almost to the edge of the river on our side. We saw they were coming directly towards us. It was absolutely perfect! We knew we had the seven once they crossed over.

They were dead. There was no doubt about it. This was our victory.

I looked to my left and reminded the ARVN next to me not to do anything until I gave the word. I buckled down, got focused and waited for the perfect time.....

Out of nowhere, the ARVN next to me stands up and yells out in Vietnamese, "It's a trap! Didi Mau!" And all hell breaks loose. The tree line immediately lights up with AK47 muzzle flashes. It is chaos at its finest. I'd imagine there were probably 45-50 VC in the tree line. There are seven of us. Take away the three ARVNs who'd just blown our cover, and now it's 50 to 4. Not good odds.

I'm processing this scene with lightning fast reaction. I see the tree line light up.

Then it all hit me at once. I immediately think, "Oh my God, this cannot be happening". I think to myself, "These guys are VC. We've been training the VC! What in the world are we doing in this village?" I'm getting my bearings straight, all the while flooded with adrenaline. My first reaction was to kill the ARVNs who'd betrayed us. This is all occurring in split second timing.

I immediately turn to my left to kill the ARVNs, who are running as fast as they can away from the scene and my M16 jams. They'd didi mau'd it out of there in a hurry. So I turned back and focused my attention on the tree line and the fire fight at hand. I'm furious, but we've got a bigger problem on our hands. We're taking heat everywhere.

I don't know how long it was, but it was a while before it calmed down. Eventually it was over, and I knew I had to get back to my men in the village. I had to warn them that the ARVNs were VC, but they were already on high alert due to the all the gunfire, so they knew something was up. I told them we'd been set up. The ARVNs we had been training were VC! We rushed back to the village and I met my men at the outskirts. In a rage, I set up 2 man assassin teams and gave the order to kill every ARVN in the entire village. Kill them all. There were seventeen of us versus one hundred useless ARVNs who were actually VC.

Let me repeat that for emphasis – THEY WERE VC.

Command's call comes in on the radio. They wanted to know what was going on as well. I was out of control, screaming at them, "You sent us in here to train the VC? These guys are VC! We've been training the VC!" They were confused of course. They were asking me what was wrong, as they had no idea what had just happened. I told command I had given the order to wipe out the village and I wasn't rescinding the offer. Everyone was dead and I wasn't changing my mind. They were accusing me of being out of my mind, but I repeated to them, "I am NOT rescinding the order!" Let's just say a lot of F bombs were dropped in that conversation! But my mind was made up.

I threw down the radio and we moved into the village.

Wouldn't you know it; the ARVNs are nowhere to be found. The village was empty, not a person in sight. I was right. They were all VC. My mind was moving at lightning speed. They could have killed us at any time. We had piles of weapons, LAWS rockets, grenades and claymores. We had to sleep sometime. But they were so stupid and useless that they didn't or couldn't do it. But the fact is we were dead as soon as we got off the truck and set foot into the camp. All of this was going through my mind. I wanted revenge. I wanted bodies. We were thrown into a meat grinder with no Intel, and we were set up from Jump Street. These were all the thoughts going through my mind at the time.

Who in the world approved this mission? They took seventeen jungle fighters who were not good with people, shoved them into a village with people who looked like the people we were killing and told us to train them. Who was the idiot who made that call? But the ARVNs were gone now, which proved everything to me. We were right. We had no business in this village to begin with. It was all a setup.

Command showed up very quickly and got us out of there in a hurry. They knew I was serious about my order and didn't want something to happen that they couldn't cover up. And like that, our journey into Pacification was over. Again, like many times before, I was never debriefed. I do know they debriefed some of my men, who obviously told them not to mess with me. They didn't. I don't think anyone talked to me for a week after that. I was completely unapproachable. There was just too much to take in. But I can tell you this; it was never discussed again after that.

Again, "The Edge" was there for me. There was so much spiritual warfare taking place in that village and I obviously did not see it. From the curses chanted on me for destroying the temples, to the demon possessed water bull, to the poisoned rice whiskey and the deadly bamboo viper – my life was hanging in the balance several times in a matter of a few short days. "The Edge" showed up in a mighty way, and it all goes back to my first day in the jungle where God honored my cry – "God help me!"

Is your life hanging in the balance? God can give you The Edge if you ask.

THE KILLING CORRIDOR

We were told we were going to be on a joint mission with several different companies we'd never worked for. There was a company already in full operation on the ground that had made contact with a full NVA force. They pulled us down from the DMZ and inserted us into the operation. This was a major sweep and the company was taking a large number of casualties.

We were located at the top of a ridge looking down into a valley. The company was attempting to push this large number of NVA (around 1,000) out of the tree line into the elephant grass at the base of the valley. From there, we'd be able to easily drop napalm on them and complete the mission. We were high on the ridge, about 300 yards from the valley so we had the high point and a great view down into the valley. It was the perfect position for the mission at hand. It was basically a big pit, and the enemy didn't know the phantoms were on their way. We had them trapped. It was a perfect killing corridor.

We were all lined up next to each other at the top of the ridge and were spraying the valley with M16s and Laws rockets. Due to our position, we were taking minimal enemy fire. It's broad daylight and it's really a good day. We're stacking the bodies and the 500lb napalm bomb is doing its job. The enemy is running along the valley to get away from the bombs, many of them on fire.

As you can well imagine, with the company pounding the tree line with napalm, the whole area is filled with heavy, billowing black smoke. It's getting harder to see the enemy due to the visibility. We're continuing to reload and fire, trying to take out as many as we could see. I'm on the ridge with the radio next to me. Junior was next to me and a few of the guys from my squad. There was a lot of chatter on the radio, as companies pass info back and forth during this very hot mission. Eventually we switched the frequency on the radio to the guy in the phantom. He was ready to drop a load and advised us that he needed a visual from us up on the ridge, as there was much movement on the ground. So we needed to pop a smoke grenade to let him know where we were.

The smoke grenades were used to prevent the VC from employing a tactic known as a false flag maneuver. The VC would attempt to draw enemy air forces into an ambush by popping standard smoke grenades, or "false flags." By using colored grenades, troops could provide air forces with a color-specific target and help them to avoid enemy ambushes. All the ground troops have to do is pop two different smoke colors and make sure their air support knows what each color signifies.

Green smoke (George) meant "friendly" and red smoke meant "the enemy".

I told him I would pop a George and let him know where our position was. So I yelled behind me to anyone who could hear, "Hey somebody pop a George", and I went back to the task at hand. A few moments later out of my peripheral vision, I see red smoke! This is not good. This mission had gone from good to bad in a split second. We were set to have a napalm bomb drop right on top of us. He's screaming in at tree top level and he's thinking we're the enemy. So at that point, it's clear that we're dead.

This is a point where your mind floods with information. You're trying to process everything that's going on all at once, in a matter of micro seconds. I see the enemy on the valley floor. I see my men alongside me on the ridge. I hear the radio chatter and gunfire. I see fire.

I see red smoke.

I hear a phantom jet coming in.

It's in that moment that time seemed to stop. That is the only way I can explain it. Perhaps it's a supernatural moment (which is what it was to me) where God makes his move. At this point, my mind is racing at supernatural speed.

I look in the distance and see the phantom coming in. He pulled his pin and the napalm bomb released and dropped from his jet. At that moment, time stopped. All I can say is that the bomb was stationary in mid-air. My mind cannot comprehend what's going on. It was a moment of disbelief. Let me tell you, your life does flash before your eyes. I'm seeing fragments of my childhood - everything.

Time stopped. I cannot get my mind around it. I'm waiting for my men to look at me and go, "Mitch, are you catching this? Are you seeing what I'm seeing?" In my mind, I'm thinking I should be hearing them say that. But no one did. But I could read "US NAVY" on the side of the bomb as clear as you can imagine. It was aimed right at me. It was going to be a chest shot. I was a dead man. Done for.

I don't know how long it was, but time began again. The bomb began moving and tumbled over our heads and exploded into the valley behind us, just barely missing us. I collected myself after this moment and I'm still trying to figure out why no one has mentioned anything about the bomb stopping in mid-air! It had to have been God performing a supernatural event. There's no other explanation for it.

Once I fully regained myself, you can imagine my adrenaline is at an all time high. I went ballistic. Someone popped the wrong smoke and nearly got us all killed. How could someone be so stupid to pop a red smoke! I screamed, "Who popped the wrong smoke?" A Marine then mentioned to me that it was a drunken Sergeant. So I tore into him. I kept hitting him with everything I had, just pounding him with every bit of rage in me. I was letting out all the frustrations of my adrenaline and near-death experience.

I left him pretty beaten and battered. After that, to me it was done. I was angry, I handled it and left it at that. After the smoke cleared, he came to me and told me that he was going to have me killed. I understand that everyone gets amped up and adrenaline is pumping during times like this, so I didn't put much mind to it. Everyone fights. It happened all the time. Threats come and go. When you're operating in a hot jungle, it's easy to get frustrated and angry. Little did I know that it would start off a war inside a war between him and me. I didn't know with his statement that he would hold to that throughout my entire tour. It was an ominous moment....haunting. After that, The Sergeant popped up time and time again, trying to get me killed (I'll speak more on that in another chapter). He was bound and determined to get me killed and after that, always tried to put me in harm's way.

But as always, God had his way and like the Killing Corridor, continued to show his grace and mercy to me throughout my time in country.

THE SERGEANT

The Sergeant was about 35 years old. I believe he was a staff sergeant. But he was a washed up individual. It was obvious he was in the Marines because he had nowhere to go. My guys and I were 18-19 years old, so he's probably twice our age and there was a division between us. Guys like that didn't get much respect in the Nam. They didn't have much rank. In the jungle, they'd approach me and tell me I'd been promoted to Corporal or whatnot and I didn't care. I didn't look at it as a lifetime thing. This guy did. But he had obviously been in for a while and was still a Sergeant. Obviously this guy had problems. You'd think that with their age, they'd be good at war. But with my contact with who I'll call "The Sergeant", I wasn't impressed. It was obvious we knew more than he did.

I'm not sure if he was accepted even by the other officers. He was just there, but like a person with no place to go. He was a drunk, like most of them were and seemed like he was going nowhere. With Hotel Company, there were probably three or four of sergeants, and we didn't trust any of them.

I met him for the first time during the Killing Corridor. Here I am yelling out "Pop a George!" as a screaming Phantom is heading our direction with a barrel of napalm and this guy pops a red. I didn't know him, but I assume he was drinking that day. He was probably pretty juiced up, and he put all our lives in jeopardy on that hill. Once I gathered myself after the traumatic experience, I went into a rage. I screamed "who popped the red?", and of course, someone said it was that drunk Sergeant. So I beat him pretty bad. I remember him saying "Mitchell, I'm gonna have you killed". After what I'd been through, it didn't carry much weight. But I logged it and put it on the back burner. My guys even asked "Want us to do him, Mitch?" (which they offered to do many times) For some reason, like all the others, I told them no. From that point, we were lifted out and we let the Army sift through the debris. Saddle up and move out. I didn't give much thought to what The Sergeant had said. He was more worried about that than I was. There were many occasions where he popped up in places, and he would not let it go.

One time in particular was, back in the States the news media didn't believe the body counts. They just couldn't fathom that we were killing so many NVA. We weren't into that. We killed as many as we could and we "stacked the bodies". We made contact all the time and it was usually us with the smaller numbers. But normally we came out pretty good. Other times, we got chewed up. So orders came down from the Pentagon to get true body counts. That meant going out immediately after a fire fight and physically counting the dead bodies. Sounds like a brilliant idea, doesn't it? If you know anything about the fighting over there, The NVA would try to drag off their dead. That wasn't to throw off our counts. That was for the funeral procession and their trip to see Buddha. For that solider, there was a send off to go to the next life. So they liked to prepare the body and send it off right. So they wanted the bodies back. They didn't like leaving them in the bush. Plus, we fought mainly at night. So imagine looking for and counting dead bodies in the middle of the night, in the middle of a war, in a jungle that was the enemy's home. Not too bright, and the last thing we were looking for. No one was taking into account that it was night and we'd just risked or lives, so there was a lot of opposition to the plan. No one wants to die for a stupid cause. But orders are orders and the sergeants and Second Louies are robots.

So the order comes down to the squad leaders after a firefight to get a body count. We were hit pretty hard that night. It's still night time, and we were all rebellious at this point. No one wants to go out and do it. It wasn't worth risking your life a second time to get a body. "If you want the bodies, go get

'em". That was our thinking. The Sergeant made his way over to my area. Junior was the squad leader at the time (he and I often traded command), so I was reporting to Junior. He bypassed Junior, came up to me and got in my face. He said, "Mitchell, I want you to go out there and get those bodies". I knew what his thinking was. He was going to get me killed. I'm sure in my own way (with a few F bombs) I told him that I wasn't doing that. He came back at me that he gave me a direct order. I still refused, after all, the order I was receiving wasn't from Junior. So I had an out. So he left frustrated. Not long after, he came back with a Captain. The Captain says to me, "Is it true he gave you a direct order and you disobeyed it?" I responded yes, that he told me to go get bodies and I refused. So he asked why. Junior mentioned to the Captain, "Sir, he didn't follow chain of command. He should have come to me." The Captain looked at the Sergeant and said "He's got me", and he walked away. The Sergeant was extremely angry at that and he walked away. So his plan for killing me blew up in his face again. Junior and I had a good laugh.

I didn't get it. He should have just left it alone, but he still had that fight on the killing corridor in his mind and wanted me dead. He never had the guts to just come shoot me himself. He was a back shooter. Now, I definitely had several opportunities to take care of him myself, and my men offered on multiple times that they'd take care of him for me. I just never took them up on it, because the killing corridor fight wasn't in the front of my mind.

The last time I saw the Sergeant was as I was preparing to leave Vietnam. I was back in the rear drinking with Junior, who was just getting ready to rotate out as he had just about finished his twelve and twenty. We had just come out of the Ashau Valley. The Sergeant had approached me a short time before and told me again that I was going to be back in the Ashau next and he would have me killed there. Normally, as I said I didn't put too much thought into his threats. This time it felt different. This time I wouldn't have Junior to watch my back. It was just going to be me and him, and it had gotten on my nerves at this point. I knew this time around it was going to either be me or him. I knew this would come to a head and one of us would be killed. Thoughts flashed in my mind as to how I would have to kill him. Maybe a firefight or a mission, a diversion and suddenly there were incoming rounds and he'd be done. I'm sure he was calculating the same, as he was pretty obvious about what he was going to do.

But I didn't want to go back to the Ashau. The Ashau scared me.

The Ashau Valley was a bad place. Eerie. There are different feels you get in the Nam. You always got a bad feeling about the Ashau. You could just feel death in the air. I operated all over and saw some bad stuff. But there was something different about the Ashau. This was really the home base so to speak of the NVA, and they knew the terrain well. There were tunnels everywhere, where they had spent years digging and hiding. This was their turf and anyone who encroached on it was in big trouble. Imagine going into Sherwood Forest and try to find Robin Hood. It was a vast, lush and rich valley; a true jungle. Triple canopy covers the whole thing, with a fog that goes up all the time. Think of the thickest part of the Amazon that has never been touched. It just feels there like nothing can breathe, especially in the heat of the day. Whenever you went in the Ashau you wanted out. It was not an area you wanted to be in. Bad things always happened in the Ashau. They didn't want us in there, and we didn't want to be there.

Luckily, a very drunk Junior and I were goofing around lifting weights and I broke my hand (which I'll discuss in another chapter) and I never had to go back to the Ashau. Again, "The Edge" was ever present, watching over me and keeping me away from death's door. I never saw the Sergeant again.

THE ASHAU VALLEY

We were somewhere up in the DMZ, and we got word that we were going to a new area that we'd never been. It was called the Ashau Valley. It's a very fertile and deep valley, vast, rich and full with NVA regulars. It was a different type of jungle than what we were used to. But the enemy liked it. I'm sure Robin Hood would have liked to have set up camp in this place. The terrain would just swallow you up. It was hard to use a map to operate because it was hard to find any recognizable markings. It was difficult to operate. I personally believe this was a base of operations for thousands of NVA. It would be a great hiding place for Osama, it was that vast. If I was in the enemy's shoes, that's where I'd be. If we were ever going to defeat the enemy there, I believe it would have taken division after division of Marines to even attempt to clear it out. Why anyone would put together a mission with a small team of Marines is beyond me, but that's where we were.

I left it up to the jungle paparazzi to brief us on the happenings in the Ashau. There was never any good news coming out of the Ashau, only bad news. When we entered the Ashau, I realized that everything I'd heard was true and more. There are certain areas you go into where there's just an eerie feeling. The enemy didn't want us there, and we could feel it. If you entered into the Ashau, you were definitely going to make enemy contact. So we expected action quickly. As the legend of Ashau became reality, we found a spot that we wanted to set up. It was the best we could do as we entered. We cleared our perimeter and a place where the choppers could land. We had plenty of access to water since there were streams nearby. It took a lot of work to clear all the trees and brush, and sometimes we had to use C4, so the enemy knew we were there.

As we're clearing, we know they're watching, plotting and scheming. They're looking at our strength and how we're setting up. Once we got set up and formed the 360, word came down that the brass wanted to set up some night patrols and listening posts. We just knew it wouldn't be good. My job was tunnel vision and I set up as best I could. I dug my hole and worked on my kill zone with the grenades, claymores and trip wires. If they were going to send waves at us, I needed to be prepared. We knew we were going to be hit, we just didn't know what their strength was.

We're on high alert and expecting some action. As we're sitting there waiting and drinking coffee (which could be your last cup at any time) around midnight, we heard sporadic laughter just outside of the perimeter. At first, I'm thinking I'm hearing something. What is going on? Is that laughter? Then I heard it louder and I starting wondering, why would they give away their position, and why would they be laughing? Well, someone smarter than me informed me they were getting all fired up with heroin. Sure enough, that's what they were doing. The NVA had brainwashed these Buddhist civilians, turned them into suicide squads and fired them up with heroin to come at us later in the night.

They had obviously told them that they were going to a better place for Buddha. This was again, part of their religious doctrine. When it came to messing up their journey, we did a good job of that. What they did was bury their dead in mound style. I guess it was to someday return to their comrades, I don't know. Our psychological with them was, when we saw those mounds, we'd dig the bodies up and mutilate them. That was a message to them, which would infuriate them. We did it as often as we could, because we found out it got to them. It didn't take long for them to put a bounty on our heads. From time to time, we'd hear on the radio with Hanoi Hannah, she'd mention us by name. We were called the "Horrible Hogs of Hotel Company", and she'd often mention us by name. She'd try to do the propaganda thing by saying a name and mentioning that your family misses you at home - something along those lines - hoping to get to us. Basically, she'd try to plant the seed that we needed to go home and get out of there. But when it came to us, she'd say that we'd be hunted down and killed. We got a kick out of it and thought, "Wow, we've really arrived here!" The best thing about it was, we'd gotten to them.

So we're waiting and listening to the laughter. We don't know how many of them there are, but they're coming. The laughter is just plain creepy. They've given away their position, but they just don't care. Their tactical plan was to send waves at us and try to break through the line at where they think the weak spots were. Sometimes if they got through, they'd dive into a foxhole and pull the pin on their grenades or satchel charges, so it was imperative that we stopped them before they got that close. They were insane, so we needed to be as well. We went to a new level of it, trying to stop the waves. Behind the waves were the hardcore regulars. Once they overrun an area, it is chaos and that squad is going to get chewed up badly. So we had to keep them in front of us.

My side of the perimeter was really hit hard by the waves. I was hitting my claymore plungers, tossing grenades and unloading clip after clip. I could tell there were many bodies in front of my hole, and it seemed like it lasted forever. Fortunately, no one got through my kill zone. But we were hit pretty hard that night. Soon, as it started getting light, the AKs stopped. But we couldn't let our guard down as we didn't know if they were going to hit us again. Medics are being yelled for as we had many wounded. Although the storm had quieted down, it was still chaos as there is a lot going on after a firefight like that. Everyone is trying to gather themselves as we'd been fighting all night. Adrenaline was still high and we're all still clamoring around.

As the sun was coming up, I'm anticipating the order to check your kill zone. If there are any wounded, you popped them a couple times in the head to make sure. Nothing is over at this point for us though, since we're still alerted to what may or may not happen. The order came down, and I grabbed my .45 to clear my kill zone. As I was heading in front of my kill zone I noticed a Marine to my right was walking into my zone. Now, I didn't know this guy as we'd rotate new guys in and out if someone was wounded, killed or sick. It happened often, especially in the Ashau. So I didn't know who he was. He obviously hadn't been there long.

I told him to get out of my kill zone. He may have said something or not heard me, I don't know. So it got physical. The unwritten rule was, don't get into someone else's kill zone. I can't explain it. I guess it had something to do with it being your personal area. You have to respect that. I mean, you set it up. If you killed the enemy, that was your trophy so to speak. So you didn't cross into someone else's kill zone. He did, so I beat him up pretty badly. I've had a bad night and I had no patience. I was still in the "crazy" state.

I head back into my kill zone to clear the bodies and not far from me I see a body. I can see that he'd been hit by shrapnel and it had taken out a large chunk of his upper thigh. He's got an RPG lying next to him, not fired. As I get closer, I realize that it's a child - a small sapper boy no older than maybe 12, still high from the heroin. I'm thinking to myself, "Oh my God, this is just a child!" I couldn't believe that someone so young would be out here. I'm looking at his eyes, as they're wide open. I'm waiting for him to blink. He sees me. He didn't say anything, but let out a small grunt. As soon as he saw my .45, his eyes got as big as saucers. I got down on my knees and straddled his chest. It was automatic - without thinking, I shot him in the face. I blew his brains out.

If you look at the mindset of the night before – the human waves and hours and hours of fighting – the constant sound of AK47 fire – the intense level of adrenaline going on for hours – maybe you can understand at that point what we were all feeling. You never know if that's going to be your last night or your last cup of coffee. You never know where the enemy is coming from our how many there are. By the time the fighting is over, you're still in that mindset – and you cannot turn it off. You're essentially crazy at that point. The state of mind is something you cannot understand until you've experienced it. You're in "kill" mode.

I see nothing but blood now. I wish from the bottom of my heart I could turn back the hands of time and not do that. It did something inside me. I broke that day. I look back and it haunts me to this day. It was a mix of regret, anger and insanity. I'd done a lot of deeds, but that one caused me to snap. I was never the same after that. To me, this wasn't war. What am I doing here? What is this war for? WHY? Yes, he was trying to kill me, but it made me even madder at the enemy. How could they fire up their own children with heroin? But you see it today with in the Middle East, where they do it all over again in the name of Allah.

I remember after that, they quickly put us in a new area and I asked immediately to run point. While walking point, I kept screaming "I didn't come here to kill kids!" That was insanity, as when you're the point, you're supposed to be quiet. But I didn't care. As I said before, something snapped in me. I was numb. I needed a team of psychiatrists at that point. My men left me alone and didn't try to stop me. Perhaps they thought I'd turn my M16 on them.

You could say, "Well, you didn't have to pull the trigger." Yes you're right. But I did, and I'm the one who lives with it every day and have lived with it since it happened. I have never been the same since that day. It's not easy to readjust. I didn't call this war. I didn't set it up. But I'm responsible for me and what I did. Now I'm in this position and I have had to deal with it for the past 40+ years. The only thing that has helped me was the grace and salvation of God. Only God can take that and heal the wound in your mind and heart. It is not like you have to forget the wound, but you have to get to a point where you can function.

I'll never get past it, but through the blood of Jesus, I have learned to cope.

TAKING COMMAND

We were operating on different missions inside Laos. They had us spread out close to where the NVA was snaking into Laos for safe haven. We knew that they were crossing the border into Laos, then back over into Vietnam and all the way down the red line. They were hitting various units and sneaking back over. So we straddled very close to this area, sending in several different recon units to pick up movement to try to find large enemy forces and look for supply lines. We knew that large NVA troop movements where going from Vietnam back into Laos and Cambodia (which was common knowledge), so the tactics and the missions involved breaking Hotel company up into several small recon units. The three to four day missions were simply to collect information and make no contact.

Three or four man units would go out for three or four days. They'd chopper us in and extract us at different extraction points. So we went in and we operated like this. We liked operating in small teams like this, because after working this way for a while, you learn to trust those working with you, and trust that they know the mission. You learned to trust the guys who you know had been in country for a while. Everyone is new at one time or another, so sometimes you do have to work with new people. But you really liked working with those who had experience for a while.

These missions had been going on for a few weeks, and there was a Second Louie who kept pressuring us to go on a mission with us. We didn't really like that, or like working with new people, since we trusted each other. We were comfortable with each other. But he had rank. He was one of those Gung Ho type officers, who seemed to want something on his war record. But he didn't have what it took, and everyone could see that. Prior to him going with us, we were in a different firefight somewhere else, and he'd lost part of his finger. He should have been Medivaced out, but he stuck around. But because of his rank and all the pressure we were under, we had no choice. We gave him plenty of signals to let him know we didn't want him along, but he ended up getting his way. We didn't feel good about it, and we didn't trust his ability in the bush. He hadn't been on any missions like this, so this whole thing is a mess to begin with.

So he pushed his rank and they reconned us out by Huey and dropped us in. On a mission like this, you just observe. You look for trails, you look for signs, but you don't move around too much. Because you're a small three to four man team, it's not too smart to give away your position when there could be a thousand NVA out there. This was their territory, and the only backup you have could be several clicks away. Help cannot come that quick. If you think about it, these were basically small suicide missions if we were not careful. So you get in a good position and watch. You try to anticipate the enemy's movements based on the terrain and base your recon on what you think the enemy would do. You look for any information you can find, take notes, shoot your grid and keep the chatter low. We'd also have to design extraction points in case something got hot. But bottom line, you stayed quiet and rarely moved. If they pick up on us, we're dead. It's that simple.

On this mission it was the Second Louie, me, Junior, Croy and a radio man, whose name escapes me. We were moving more than normal this time because the Second Lieutenant was with us. He wanted to move around too much. We were on patrol rather than recon it seemed. We were totally exposed and none of us liked it. We were pissed off, since he was putting the whole mission in jeopardy. I honestly don't think he understood what we were to accomplish. So we were deep into Laos, and possibly deep in trouble due to our excessive movement. As we looked for signs, we came across fresh tank tracks.

The entire area was mowed down. Now, one thing you need to realize is, when you see tank tracks, that means a lot of NVA. This is a force that's pretty big if they're rolling tanks through there.

So the Second Lieutenant, instead of thinking about his next move, informs us that we're going to follow the tank tracks.

That was not our mission! Our mission was to take the information, shoot the grid and report this back to Hotel. To follow these tank tracks was absolutely suicide. There was no way to know how many tanks or how many of the enemy there were! We're ready to leave now.

Immediately after he said that, we huddled up Three Stooges style (which was a little bit of humor on this crazy mission) and one of my men said, "Let's kill him Mitch". Now, normally I would have gone with the suggestion, as he was putting our lives in jeopardy. I didn't know where it came from, and I give God credit for that idea, but split-second, I said, "No, let's take his command away." That's a no-no. Unheard of. It's mutiny. You don't take someone's command away in the Marine Corps. You're facing a court martial, my men are facing a court martial - that will get you thrown into the brig real quick. You just don't do it. The only way I could see getting away with it is if you were in battle conditions and in front of many witnesses, and it's proven that the one in command has clearly lost his mind. We didn't have that. If it was weighed out in any Military court, we'd have been screwed. So, I don't know what made me think of doing that, but I did. I don't know if that Second Louie made it out of Vietnam, but if he lived through it, he's alive because of what I did for him (and I owe it to God), because my men were definitely going to pop him. Our adrenaline is flowing, and we're all screaming inside "Let's GO!" I'm sure there was a huge force of NVA. We're a small force, and we maybe have water for three days and some rations. We had plenty of ammo, but no Laws rockets. Nothing to take on a large

NVA force. Like I said, suicide. We were dead if we would have gone with his orders. So we were at 100% "pop this guy".

I put my M16 under his chin and informed him that we were taking away his command. My men and I took his command, tied his hands behind his back and he starts falling apart. He was crying and wailing, as I'm sure he heard my men ask to kill him - which brought an entirely different problem. Is this guy gonna fight us? Is he gonna start screaming and make noise and give away our position? Basically, he's now a POW and we're a long way from our extraction point. So we didn't know what to expect. Not only that, we still had tank tracks! Who knew what was coming down the line? We didn't know, but we did know there were a lot of NVA out there. So my men went with it. We hopped on the radio and told Hotel that the Second Louie had lost his mind, that he had Malaria or something and we needed to move up the extraction point. The Louie is running a fever, so we need an extract right now.

We get on the chopper, and I'm expecting this guy to just spill the beans and we'd all be in trouble. I knew he wouldn't say anything on the chopper, since it was always loud, but I knew as soon as we got to the rear I was in for it. What was funny was, on board the chopper my men and I are eyeballing each other, with kind of a smug look on our faces. We're not talking, but we're smiling and laughing after realizing the impact of what just happened. Just the idea that we took the command away from this guy after what we were sure was death, kind of hit us. We got on board and were finally safe. But he asked to go on the mission, and he got what he asked for.

When we got back to the rear, he didn't say anything. They met us back on the perimeter where the chopper landed and took him away. I made my way back to my area and just waited for them to come get me. My gut told me I was done. I figured it'd be a matter of time before a bunch of MPs with M16s came for me and threw away the key. But they never did. Again, it had to be God at work. We dodged a bullet and he dodged a lot, because we would have killed him and left him there. No one ever came to me and asked me to explain myself. I know they choppered him back to a medical facility, because keep in mind he'd lost part of his finger earlier. But I never saw him again. None of us were ever questioned on the mission. No one ever said a word to me about it. It had to have been the grace of God.

JOY LOST AT THE RIVER – "THE EDGE"

We had been humping all day inside Laotian border. There were four companies on the move, which is over a thousand Marines snaking through the jungle in column formation. Marines for well over a mile. It apparently was a very important mission, as command flew in a Captain for this one. This Captain flew in with a full entourage, including a bald, personal cook along with an NBC camera crew, which is nothing but excess baggage on a combat mission.

At this point we had not refilled our canteens and we're very much in need of some water. We were all exhausted, frustrated, hot and thirsty. Our patience was running thin. We were coming into an area where we could hear a river, so it made us thirstier. We were in a thick brushy area along a trail. We couldn't see the river, but we could hear it.

We were about eighty yards from the point of the column and were about to stop for the night. We needed about an hour and a half to clear our area, dig in and get some food and water. We didn't form a perimeter this time. We stayed in column formation, which left us at a weaker strength and at more of a defensive posture and offensive. We waited for the call to come over the radio to stop, and while we were still moving when we heard the "pop pop" of an M16. This is not too unusual. I figured the point man had an itchy trigger finger or something, so I wasn't on high alert since I didn't hear an AK.

Then a call came over the radio to stop, set up and fill canteens like nothing happened.

So we didn't think anything out of the ordinary.

So we were sitting on the ground, stopped and relaxed. Junior told me it was my turn to go fill canteens. That meant taking twenty or so canteens, tying them to a rope and dragging them down to the water's edge to fill. You packed light, with an M16 and a bandolero maybe. Everyone had their turn, and this time it was mine. Well, I didn't want to go. So we talked back and forth,

"Not me! It's your turn Mitch, you do it!"

"Look I'll do it the next two times if you go this time."

"NO way!"

"Ok, let's say it is my turn. If you go, I'll give you some peaches or poundcake!"

I was wearing him down and he finally gave in. So Junior took as many on the rope and took off up the trail towards the river. Normally, the Captain would send a couple squads to set up security across the river (very slowly) into the tree line to protect the men as they filled the canteens. Unfortunately, and for reasons I still don't understand, they didn't do that this time. That meant the men were exposed. The force that was supposed to set security was obviously lazy, as we'd been humping all day. That was a major error, and it cost us dearly that day.

So Junior was gone maybe twenty minutes or so, and all hell breaks loose. I'm looking around my area trying to determine if it's coming near my area. RPGs, mortars and AK fire is going all around us. Your first thought is "OH F!" But I didn't see any action around me. There is chaos and chatter on the radio telling us to hold our position and stay away from the river. But my first thought was Junior, and it was supposed to be me down there filling canteens! I didn't want to go to the river, but now I had to. I grabbed my M16 and grabbed as many bandoleros as I could. I started running towards the river. As I'm moving up the column, Marines are telling me, "Hey you're going the wrong way! They said not to go to the river!" I responded "Don't I know it!" So I get as close to the point as possible and on the trail I see a big tree with two NVA tied to it, dead. These were the two pops I heard earlier. To the right, I then see the stacks of rice and weapons with fires still going. I'm thinking, "Oh my God. We've come across an NVA base camp." My adrenaline is pumping now. To my left, I see Marines coming up an incline from the river, bleeding and shot. It's pure chaos at this point.

I move to my left and my plan was to get to the river and scream for Junior. I hit the incline and slid down to the bottom of the river. I can only describe it as like a water slide. With the water, blood and mud in the mix, before I could set any strategy, I slid down and shot into the river. As soon as I hit the river there was a giant rock at the bottom. It was the only one in the river, which I now refer to as my "Edge". God obviously was protecting me. The rock allowed me protection from incoming enemy fire, and allowed me to scan the position without taking rounds. I see bodies of Marines all around me, riddled with bullets. Many of them were dead, many were wounded. It was so loud too. I couldn't scream for Junior with all the gunfire, RPGs and mortar round noise. I knew I had to get out of there. I knew I was dead. All I could do was return fire. I kept my eyes on the tree line, looked for smoke or muzzle flash and pointed in that direction. I emptied clip after clip. I'm screaming at the Marines behind me to give cover fire. I started moving towards wounded in the water. But as soon as I'd get close, the enemy would hit them with rockets or gunfire. They were toying with me. I was able to rescue a few, but the majority was getting hit as I got to them. But I kept coming back to the rock....the Edge. It kept me safe.

My M16 kept jamming, and I tossed it away. I screamed behind me for another. This kept happening over and over. My M16 would jam and I would toss it away and scream for another. At that point, the Captain screamed at me "Marine, don't throw those weapons away!" My mind filled with anger. I don't recall his name, but I blame him for what happened that day. Had he seen what I had seen moving up the column, we would have protested. Why would you send men to fill canteens when you stumble upon an NVA base camp? But with the mother lode of rice and weapons we found, along with the fires going and two NVA tied to the tree, he had to have seen it. How could you not see that? We were all sitting ducks. Marines were getting killed and all because this idiot of a Captain didn't follow procedure. It enraged me. I screamed back at him, "You won't live through the night! This is all your fault!" Well, that night, they choppered him out.

I turned back around and to my left, I see a man just standing in the water on our side. I'm screaming at him, wondering why he's not doing anything. I tell him to give me some cover fire and give me some help. I turn behind me and tell someone to give him a bloop gun. Someone gave him one I screamed at him for cover fire. It was clear he didn't know anything, as he fired it directly into the water, exploding shrapnel everywhere. It's like a grenade exploding in front of me. I'm screaming at him again, furious. I'm surprised that I didn't just pop him right there for nearly killing me. From behind me, I hear someone yelling to me, "He's NBC! He's a cameraman!" They pulled him back into the tree line for obvious reasons.

I had a friend who came along with us on a few occasions. He was a short guy, and we called him "Little Bit". Little Bit was a source of joy for me in the bush, as he was a really funny guy. When you have death and destruction all around, you welcome the times when you can laugh and joke. Little Bit was that to me. I don't remember where I met him, but I remember how often he made me laugh. I looked again to my left and saw Little Bit face down in the river about 20 yards from me. He'd been shot in the neck, but was still alive. I knew I had to get to Little Bit. But since the enemy had been playing games with me with the other wounded, I knew I had to wait a short time before I could try to get him out. I eventually timed it, and moved from behind the rock towards Little Bit. I didn't get but a few feet from him and they hit him with an RPG. At that point they took what "little bit" of joy I had in the jungle. I snapped mentally. It was just too much to take on. I do remember taking what was left of his body and passing it up the bank to the Marines behind me. A short time after that, it was all over, as I'm sure the enemy knew that the phantom jets and artillery were coming.

I made my way back to my area, knowing full well Junior was dead. But thank the Lord, there he was. I breathed a sigh of relief. But there was nothing to jump up and down about. We lost a lot of men that day, including my friend Little Bit. There was no victory that day. We just had to keep moving. We could not allow ourselves to be overtaken with grief and despair, or soon we would be dead too. So I could not grieve for Little Bit the way I needed to.

I was awarded the Navy Commendation Medal for that mission. The official statement reads "At a river near Khe Sahn". But as I said, it was Laos, which they couldn't revel to the public at the time.

But I always go back to the rock. The only one in the whole river, and I happened to land behind it. God gave me The Edge that day. Looking back, I had the edge all along, and he showed me the edge several times throughout my tour. I thank the Lord for giving me "The Edge".

In Vietnam, it's safe to say that everyone needs some kind of an edge because of the tactics and enemy of the war. Everything seems to be against you. Whatever edge you can muster up or comes your way, you sure take advantage of it.

In November 2010 God reminded me of the rock in the river. Basically as he speaks to me, he said, "Have you considered the possibilities that in that ambush, where you shot into the river, there just happened to be the most welcome rock in your life? At the right time and the right place?"

Because of the mix of blood and mud of those coming out of the river, it was very slippery at the incline to the river. When I hit it, the plan was to ease down to the river edge, peek out and see if I could find Junior. It didn't work out like that, as everyone was telling me I was going the wrong way. But I had to go as it was my destiny.

Because of the all the mud and blood, this slippery goo created the ride of my life into certain death. God, who is my rock, my fortress and deliverer knew exactly what I needed to give me the edge - the refuge I needed in this time of life and death troubles and battles.

Have you considered the rock?

I immediately knew I had to dig deeper, because numerous times I flash back to this day and remember that there was only one rock (like my rock) that was there as I shot into the river. As far as I could see, there was no rock like my rock. In Hebrew the word rock means "refuge" or "edge".

Wow…An edge.

That day the rock was exactly what I needed. That day the enemy was coming at me like a flood and God raised up a standard – the edge. Suddenly my destiny mixed with God's faithfulness, showed that I had a God who had it well in hand as the battle raged in the natural and supernatural. Many were taken out that day. God spared me.

What I leave with you is this: God is your rock and refuge – your edge too. When the enemy comes in to kill, steal and destroy, rise up for you have a rock, an edge, and his name is Jesus! So be confident in the truth. You have the rock, the edge no matter what battle you're in. You have the edge, which is more than enough.

1 Samuel 2:2 says - There is no one holy like the Lord; there is no one besides you; there is no Rock like our God.

That pretty much says it all right there.

THE SAPPER BOY

We'd been operating up North, perhaps even in the Ashau Valley. Not too sure, as we'd been moving a lot.

After a while you learn the area you're in. There are signs as you set up a perimeter. To start, you'd set up day patrols. We were set to make contact, so we had to be prepared. As whoever gets the orders to go out, you're gonna send off from the 360 several different patrols that won't interconnect on the grid, but work off the 360. That way you're sweeping the entire area. Those who don't go out, are spread out on the perimeter to eliminate holes. You'd go out, determine where contact was made and pinpoint where they were planning to attack. Then you'd set up your perimeter accordingly.

At the time, our patrols had been hit pretty good, so we knew the enemy was flush in the area. What the enemy would do was wound a few here or there. Hit a bit here, a bit there but they'd never tip their hand as far as their strength. It's because they were planning a night move. Periodically as well, they'd send in mortar rounds. They were very good at that. They knew we'd be looking for the flash, so they'd pop ten rounds in a tube and move. They know you'd call in 155s or 175s and hit that grid real hard. But they were always one step ahead. They'd hit us and flee. So we could never know how deep they were. Were they rogue teams or a thousand of them? Your guess was as good as mine. But we were in their area, and they had many underground tunnels that could hide several thousand. So we never knew. We just had to make sure our 360 was tight, because if they crossed the wire, we were in deep trouble.

We knew we were in a bad area. So top priority was to shore up your kill zone. Claymores are out, you have grenades in your hole with you, Constantine wire - so you know right where they're at. You basically set up as many traps as you can. You were responsible for your own kill zone. Right before the sun goes down, sometimes we'd have to do night patrols. We hated them. They were the most dangerous, but those were the orders. The order of business is, we go out and set up in areas where we think they may be. Kind of like a listening post, but more of an ambush opportunity. That way we knew just where they were.

That night, you could feel something bad was going to happen. It was surreal. You could cut it with a knife. We made contact earlier and didn't know how many of them. It happened to be overwhelming numbers, but we didn't know at the time. The VC had fired up several of their people with heroin. It's about 12-1 o'clock in the morning, and tensions were high. The adrenaline rush that night was huge. In my area there happened to be major waves. And it seemed like they sent them all towards me.

The strategy is, if they can get through to the center of the hill, they have the opportunity to take us all out. In my kill zone, I know what's going on, so I can't turn around and spray. That's how we all were. So we had to keep them in front of us. They sent the first wave with children and older folks. How someone could juice up their kids with heroin is beyond me, but we've also seen those same suicide bombers in Iraq and Afghanistan. I don't understand it. But that's what they would do.

So they're coming in waves and I'm hitting the claymore plungers and unloading clip after clip. They keep coming. Some of them are hitting their satchel charges early because they're doped up, hung up in the wire and excited. From the wire to my hole was probably 20-30 feet, so they were close. I can hear them too, because they would scream and laugh as they came towards us. It was total chaos. There were bodies peppering the area in front of my hole. I know they're climbing over the wire and it's nuts. During the explosions, you are able to see silhouettes of how many numbers are coming your way. Your mind is in such a state of chaos because you don't know really when it's going to be over. So your goal is to take care of your kill zone and make it through the night until the sun comes up.

But I know if I stop for one second, they're going to get to me. So I have to keep the intensity. We were spread very thin, but no excuse, we have to go to work. Fortunately the human wave that was coming at me was very high, so they weren't firing much. But none the less, they keep coming. They're not only hitting my area, but also various spots in the 360. But you have to keep focused on your area and not worry about what's behind you. It's a scary thought. But I had to make sure no one got through my kill zone.

One of the hardest things is, when it happens that large, a lot of the guys in our perimeter are getting wounded. But you can't leave your position. If they over run the position, it's over. The medic, if he's still alive has to make the rounds. If you get hit, you gotta keep going. Luckily, your adrenaline is so high that you are able to keep going unless it's something major.

As the dawn's coming in, the adrenaline flow is still high. On this 360, I didn't know who was on my right. New people are always coming in, so you seldom make friends. So there was a new guy on my right. So I'm looking in front of me and there are bodies everywhere. Bodies on the wire, blood and guts. Quite a mess. So we received orders - "saddle up, we're moving out. Kill all the wounded". When the time came for me to go out and clear my area, this new guy walks in to my kill zone. Well, that's not something you did there. You take care of what's in front of you. So I tell the guy to stay out of my kill zone. He must not have known. It led to a fight and I beat him pretty good. I hate to use the word "trophy", but when you're in that state of mind, that's what it is. I was protective of my kill zone. Those were my bodies and everyone else needed to stay away.

I can't explain my thinking at the time. I can't. The firefights, the screaming, the blood - and you see that over and over again.

When you're in the Nam, you flash in and out of who you are. When I got there, I wasn't ready for the war. Wasn't even prepared. But then you get dialed into war and you change. It just does something to you. Your mind is not in the right place, that's all I can say. You'd have to go through what we all went through to understand.

So I made it down the hill further and was surprised to see a little boy, maybe 10 years old who was one of the sappers. He'd been hit on the hip with some shrapnel, which had taken a pretty big chunk out of his upper thigh. Off to his right, I saw he had an RPG that he didn't fire, obviously because he was very high on heroin. He'd made it pretty far, which surprised me. At the time, I carried a .45 pistol and I had it out. My job was to make sure that every wounded one in my area was eliminated. As I approached him, I'm standing over him, thinking to myself "My God this kid's young!" When he saw me, his eyes got as big as saucers. He didn't talk, but only let out a small groan. But his eyes were talking. They were saying "don't do this".

I didn't even think about what I was doing. I pointed my gun and shot him in middle of the face with my .45. His brains exploded everywhere. Something broke inside. That kill did something to me. I had done a lot of bad things up to that point, but nothing I'd done had hit me like this. This was a young kid. As soon as I pulled the trigger, I wished I could turn back the clock. I didn't even check on the other bodies. I just walked away. This deeply bothered me. I couldn't just move onto the next mission. I couldn't just get it out of my head. I got mad.

Why was he here in the first place? What's he doing in this war? It made no sense. My mind flooded with all of it. Like I said, something broke. I had snapped. I walked screaming "I didn't come here to kill kids!"

Part of me died that day. I wasn't the same gung ho jungle fighter I had become.

I wish I hadn't have done it. I can't change it. But it gripped me, and still grips me to this day. You see it over and over again. His eyes haunt me. They beg me, "Please don't". That particular instance has had such an impact on me, and I have never been the same. I have not gotten over it and will never get over it. No peace. No resolve. But through the grace of God and forgiveness in Jesus Christ, I am still trying to cope.

ROTATING OUT

We had just returned from the Ashau Valley, where we'd been hit pretty hard by the human waves I mentioned before. Returning to the rear was much needed, as we'd been out for quite some time and needed to resupply and rest for a bit. Junior got his orders that he was rotating out. I knew that now I would have no one to watch my back against this Sergeant who was still trying to kill me. He hadn't let up at all. He told me again when we hit the rear that when we returned to the Ashau Valley, I wouldn't be coming back. He was going to have me killed out there.

Out of all the times my life had been in danger, nothing felt like this one. I'd ignored his repeated threats for quite some time now. But this was different. I knew I was in for it. I just knew he'd have me killed if he got the chance. I didn't want to just kill him outright. But I knew I would have to. It was going to be me or him. This was when Junior came up with a bright idea to help me with my problem.

My time was short. I imagine I had but only a few weeks before I rotated out, so any risk now would be death for sure. When you are down to counting days, you usually stayed in the rear until your orders to leave came. But this Sergeant was planning on taking me on my final mission. Sometimes we make decisions that are painful any way we go, but God can direct it to bring life from pain.

Junior suggested we go lift weights and burn off steam. So we went over to the workout area, where everyone would lift weights. But first, we had to get good and drunk. What a brilliant idea. Let's get completely wasted and lift weights! Well, it wasn't long before the effects of alcohol and lack of focus reared their ugly heads. I'm still not quite sure how it happened. One minute I'm pushing up weight and the next minute my hand is split wide open and I could see the bones. I immediately got faint and felt sick from the trauma.

Junior quickly commandeered a jeep and took me over to the medic, and of course no one believed our story due to the severity of my hand. As they bandaged my hand and prepped to send me out, Junior and I ran into whom else but the Sergeant. He asked us where we were going, to which I replied while holding my hand up, "I'm shippin' out Sarge!" Junior reminded him that we wouldn't be going back to the Ashau. I wish I could describe the look on his face! It was worth all the pain and misery. Not long after that, they shipped me to Yokosuka Naval Hospital and from there I received my orders to go home.

This scripture reminds me of that situation and the protecting hand of God:

"Romans 8:28-31 – And we know all things work together for good to them that love God and are called according to his purpose. For whom he did foreknow, he also did predestinate to be conformed to the image of his son that he might be the firstborn among many brethren. Moreover, whom he did predestinate, he also called, and whom he called he also justified, and whom he justified, he also glorified. What shall we say to these things? If God is for us, who can be against us?"

Indeed. Who can stop what God has ordered?

JUNIOR

I had just dug in on the perimeter and I was cooking my dinner. But I don't think C Rations (especially pork steak) should ever be considered for the last meal of the day.

We had been humping all day and the usual set up is to dig my spot on the 360.

Everyone had to clear their kill zone and design whatever lethal traps they could. Because of the time element, many times, I would cook with C-4, because it was quick and would kill whatever organisms that may do me harm. It was on one of these types of scenarios when I was cussing my pork steak (which was a daily event), and I look up to see a Mexican looking fellow. He threw me a bottle of hot sauce and told me that it would help kill off the horrible taste of what I was eating. The hot sauce was extremely hot, but over time I became addicted to it. Then hot sauce was the edge I needed to kill the microorganisms in the nasty C Rations they'd provide us.

That Mexican looking guy was actually Puerto Rican, and we became the best of friends. His name was Gaspar Gonzalez, but we all called him Junior. Junior and I would get together often for dinner out in the jungle, and he would always bring the hot sauce. Getting close to someone is not something you tried to do or wanted to do. Because too many times one or both are not around long. Junior and I just happened, and I'm forever grateful. My time with Junior and our friendship was special. So many things stand out about him, his kindness and friendship; and there was a soft side about him, which was rare to see in the middle of a war. I don't know exactly when I snapped in the Nam, but my guess it was early on. I had come full circle since my first day in the bush. I definitely malfunctioned as my Marine Corps training failed to kick in right away.

The turn around came soon enough, as we were piling dead gooks in a fire base up North. I wanted to take a break, since stacking bodies in the hot sun called for some lunch. I wasn't one to eat with other Marines, so I decided to eat my lunch at the top of the pile of bodies. A couple of other Marines joined me. It seemed appropriate at the time, due to the night we'd had before. If it had gone the other way, perhaps they'd be eating fish and rice on our dead carcasses. So go the spoils of war. Sometimes, you just have to reward yourself. Now, this may sound crazy, but while we were eating, some Marines decided it was a Kodak moment. After finishing our lunch, Marines are anxious for the photo shoot to begin. The range of shots included me with two dead gooks' heads under each of my arms. One of the Marines gave me the film and told me, "This will mean more to you than me." I sent the film home to my parents, telling them to develop them and hold them until I got back. I never mentioned to my parents what the pictures were all about. Well, they were horrified, as they should have been. My mindset at the time was not sharp enough to realize what this type of carnage would do to them.

Fortunately I had a friend in Junior, who began writing my mother to help with damage control. I believe in a weird sort of way, whatever I wrote to my parents was therapy for me. Time after time, Junior would soften the blow and downplay the events like a good politician. He tried his best to form misdirection plays and deflect the focus off of me and my crazed mind. In the jungle, we didn't have time to write. But Junior would make the time to write my mother and try to salvage what he could. That's a side of Junior I want everyone to know and appreciate. Junior, in so many ways adapted to this war in a unique way. From that point on, my mother would write Junior more than she would me. But under the circumstances, she felt more at ease, and she should have been.

Because I was so close to the same hell as he was, I didn't see the war taking a heavy toll on him. Junior was up to his eyeballs in helping me. When bullets were flying, Junior was dialed in, focused and never got emotional as he held it all in, only to explode time and time again in the future, as I have recently learned. One situation I remember with Junior was when we were deep out on a mission. Our radio was blowing up with chatter that a large NVA force was closing in to intercept our position. Word came down to set up where we were stopped, and we'd take them as they come. I saw around us that there was no cover and no time to dig in. We were in elephant grass, so visibility was terrible. I remember having some sort of panic attack, since our conditions gave the edge to the NVA. However, God intervened in a supernatural way, and The Edge remained steadfast. Junior on the other hand, was not fazed at all. With his half smile, he said to me, "We're good right here." Rather than look at him and tell him he was crazy, I was taken by his confidence in an impossible situation. The intel we received was precise and specific, telling us there were thousands. Maybe there were hundreds, but that was more than what we had.

It was early afternoon. Normally a head on broad daylight assault is unusual. The numbers coming at us were huge. There was no time to call in a fire mission, because they were quickly upon us. Junior and I were crouched in the elephant grass waiting for the end. I don't know what the other Marines were doing, as the elephant grass stops all lines of sight. It was a perfect setting for friendly kills, as again, visibility was lousy and the kill zones were limited. Junior and I remained silent as we tried to anticipate how many would come our way. A force that size just could not disappear and I remember hearing someone say, "We're screwed" over the radio. I can only give God the credit that day, because it was one of those God moments where there is absolutely no other explanation other than a "God thing". I had a lot of respect for Junior, but that day took it to a new level as my friend helped me hold it together and we made it out alive.

I go back to the time at "The River", when it was my turn to refill the canteens. Many would question who keeps track of turns, as there are soldiers who do that. They always know whose turn it is to walk point, go on night patrol or whose turn it is to carry the Starlight scope. I remember starting to work on Junior, "Please go for me and I will do it the next ten times. " Junior said no until I exhausted myself and was even begging. Finally he broke. Yes it was all somewhat of a game, but there was an underlying goodness to him that only a few of us got a glimpse of. He was as exhausted and just as spent as the rest of us was, but he went anyway. I remember calm not long after he left, as things went silent. Then I heard the bassy boom of the AK47s firing at the river. I remember thinking that I had to go to the river, as my friend was there and it should have been me. I remember as I was running towards the river, soldiers were telling me I was going the wrong way. I knew I was, but I had to get to my friend, Junior.

After many events, I made my way back to my unit, still not knowing if Junior had made it. When I saw his full smile, I was so glad and relieved to see that Puerto Rican face! I had said some things that day at the river to the one in charge of that disaster. I think in part, payback came in the form of our squad being told to take point and cross the river the next day. We'd pounded the other side of the river that night with everything from a fire base close by. The enemy anticipated this tactic and pulled back to an underground position. We knew there would be contact the next day. Just getting in that river again wasn't pleasant, let alone going across. We made our way into the tree line and began to set up for an online assault. Once again, everyone is in position and they opened up on us. Junior was to my left and he went down as an AK47 round hit his knee. I immediately went to help him, and as I turned towards him an AK47 round hit me across the right eye and I went down with Junior. Luckily, it wasn't a direct hit for him or me. I remember looking up to the sky and screaming, "I'm blind!" which wasn't the case. Later as we're sitting together, still bleeding and covered with battle dressings, we began to laugh at each other. Most of the joy was the fact that we were both ok. That's what mattered, because others paid a full price that day. I thank God for the edge.

During our tours of Vietnam, we were very close as far as our rotating out. We were both short at the time, meaning we didn't have much time left before we rotated out. But one must always remember that just one day in the bush could be final. The worst crime is to be killed as a short timer, but it happened time and time again. We tried to help the shorts by taking them off missions and assignments, but seasoned Nam killers were a hot commodity. The military up the chain could not care less about the shorts. Relief only came when bucu gooks went on their journey to the afterlife.

Junior and I put together a plan for R&R. It was time and our travel agent (us) picked Bangkok for a five day extravaganza. Getting our R&R at the same time was near impossible, because with Junior and me gone at the same time, it left 3 Charlie vulnerable with holes. We would have gone anyway, and I think the brass knew it too.

We needed a break from the insanity. We were both messed up, and when you're messed up, you don't notice it. You're surrounded by insanity and chaos, and that becomes normal. Trust me when I tell you that we were both in need of a rest. So we took off on our five day R&R to Bangkok. I must say, Junior and I had a blast. From day one, Bangkok got fat with war vets traveling to party. The scheme was simple; take in the soldiers, give them pleasures beyond anything they can think of, separate them from their cash and send them back on their way broke but satisfied so they would go back to Vietnam with tales that would rival Sodom and Gomorrah.

As soon as we were in country at the airport, we were welcome and warned at the same time not to get too crazy. Maybe for some that was a green light. Junior and I had simple plans that involved good food, beer and women. We soon arrived at our air conditioned hotel with an emphasis on "air conditioned". Air conditioning was huge and we enjoyed ever moment of it. Both of us had dreamed of a bath. Not just a bath, but a full service bath. As soon as we got to our rooms and dropped our bags on the floor, we got a knock on the door and soon began our negotiations, as many or few, with the hotel whore. The bath was great, however I stopped with just a bath, as we planned on going out to the club later and I wanted to see all the girls. We each hired a taxi driver for the week. My driver wore at least two hats, as he was my photographer as well. He would be stationed outside my door until I said go home. The clubs were unlike I had ever seen. Since I was 19, I hadn't been to clubs anyway. I was not old enough, and that should beg the question – If I'm old enough to fight for my country, shouldn't I be old enough to drink a beer? I guess I'll leave that for the smart people who make the rules.

Outside on the street corners, customers could view some of the Thai prostitutes as they lounged on pillows wearing numbers and skimpy outfits. We couldn't wait to go inside. Inside, there were many more choices, and we were both gridlocked. Each of us had to come up with a number. Fortunately, they had a test drive program for the confused. The clubs offered a huge dance floor. So you'd find a table, order some drinks and tell the waiter or waitress that you'd like to speak to Number 45, let's say. She would come to your table, talk, drink or dance and whatnot. They key was to make your decision early, because we were pretty drunk with the "tiger piss" they were serving us. I found a girl early on who I liked named Toi Singtarosi, or at least that's what she said her name was. We were together the whole five days. She was a hustler and she had her own agenda. She owned a beauty salon and whatever you could want, she had the connection. For example, if you wanted Thai sticks packaged, she had you covered; "No problem G.I."

Junior and I decided that we needed weapons, or at least a pistol. She put us together with a small arms dealer and he had a .357 magnum with a holster. I thought it would be great to take back to the jungle. I tried to get a money wire from back home,

as I was spending a lot of money. The other foolish expenditure were some tailored suits, as my plan was to come back to Bangkok and marry Toi – talk about out of my mind! Junior was a lot more grounded and simply stayed in party mode. I stayed in "Have you lost your mind?" mode. For five days Junior and I enjoyed the Thai food and especially the hot sauce that was so hot it closed off my throat from the swelling. I asked Toi to bring me the hottest sauce her country had to offer, and boy did she deliver. I remember it was clear like Vodka and came in a little shot glass. All I know is that a little went a long way, and I got addicted to it. Junior was not a fan. Why was I always attracted to things that would hurt me? I surely do not know! But we had the best time of our lives. It all went by as a blur, but we sure got everything we'd asked for with all the trimmings. Soon it was time to refocus on the war, which was our reality. We'd have to leave our fantasy.

Junior was a unique soldier and hard to put in a box. I never really understood him because he never let anyone in close. Even I was never let in, but I know we had something special. We were brought together in that hell called Vietnam, and the toll on each of us was different. I never knew and I don't know today who Junior was for. I'm not even sure he was for himself. He never gave me much, but everyone wanted to know what he was about. Junior was so smart with maps and shooting grids and knowing where we were. But he showed very little emotion.

We were in a hot area once, and Junior put out a listening post to give us an early warning. We'd been hit hard the night before with waves. We had no contact from them and I went with him to check on guys on the LP. We thought they were dead, since no one had responded. When we found them, they were asleep, not dead. Without warning, Junior took the butt of his M16 and he began to crush this Marine's skull. At first I stayed out of it, but it took everything I had no to step in. He was killing the guy. It was a strange moment out of nowhere. I had never seen Junior so upset. That Marine was medevaced out, with a guarantee that he'd never sleep on a Lima Papa again.

Junior awoke a bit that day, and it was not pretty. I never talked to him about it.

Junior and I had just come out of the Ashau Valley. They choppered us into the rear to regroup and recover. This was rare, but the Ashau ranks high on the least attractive sectors in the Nam. It took everything. It only offered up darkness and death. The NVA didn't want to share the Ashau with anyone. So the Sergeant popped up again telling me that he was going to get me killed in the Ashau. Well, not long after that, Junior was given a gift and the timing was over the top. He was rotating out. His orders had just come through. I was happy for him, but at the same time I would really miss him. I knew I had to kill the Sergeant now, since I knew I'd be dead soon – rotting in the Ashau. The only choice was to get really drunk, both in celebration of Junior's out and either mine or the Sergeant's demise. It was then where we came up with

"Operation Broken Hand".

As far as my best friend, Gaspar Gonzales, Jr., I leave it here:

No words can describe our friendship in the Nam. I will definitely be coming to see you, my friend, because you cannot come to see me. Rest in peace Junior, until we meet again.

"PERCEPTIONS FROM A JUNGLE GRUNT"

My thoughts for this chapter is "Hindsight is 20/20", and I am definitely certified 0311 as my MOS. The US and most countries have an unlimited supply of Men, women and children to feed the war machine. The common denominator on the supply side is economics. There are many scenarios I can give you. Coming from a large, poor white family was the main driver for joining the Marine Corps. I wanted to go to college. At 18 I graduated high school mid-term, which fit right into my plans. I wasted no time as I tucked my diploma away and headed for the recruiting station in downtown Indianapolis. "I'm really gonna do it this time, mister" was my attitude. So before I could give this serious thought, in a whirlwind of physicals and swearing in, I belonged to Uncle Sam in the blink of an eye. Keep in mind, this was 1968 and there weren't a lot of people heading to the recruiting station. They were heading to Canada to escape the draft.

I did not examine the big picture, which was what is this war about? Where is Vietnam on the map? Why do these people (our so called enemy) need to be killed? I should have watched a bit more Walter Cronkite as the Hueys were choppering out the wounded and dead. I knew when joining for two years, I was certainly headed to Vietnam. There was no time for school now. My world view at the time was mainly focused on the East side of Indianapolis. I had a narrow view and limited information to make a life and death decision. Everyone I knew was in school. Those I knew who weren't had no plan. Things were getting heated across the country with the protests and the Tet Offensive was launched. Ready or not I'm going to Vietnam. For how long was yet to be determined. Let the tour begin. It's Twelve and Twenty – twelve months and twenty days.

Looking back, what is clear to me is, War is a smorgasbord of opportunity for multi-national corporations who have a need to feed in a war torn country. Their appetites are enormous. They are there to ravage the banquet table. When the best parts are consumed, they leave the mess for someone else. They are loyal to nothing except the dollar. On the table is an endless serving of pain, suffering and death, just like a Great White shark tearing into a pod of baby seals. The takeout by these greedy corporations would make the Vikings proud. This banquet involves everyone in country, invited or not. The multi-national corporations preparing the toxic stews and munitions of death have one thing in mind, and that is profit. The profiteers of war can be found in household names like Dow and Monsanto and the lists who participate in this frenzy to get their share. The other usual suspects can be linked to helicopters, 5.5s, 6mm ammo, .50 cal, M16 manufacturers, bomb manufacturers, and so on. The secret chefs of war who prepare lethal portions that sometimes just poison those who don't know the food poison got them too, and they were just servers only. Many of the chefs want to remain secret, but their mess that includes over 58,000 American deaths and millions of Vietnamese.

The menu of war has its own specialty dishes. Vietnam's main course was Agent Orange coupled with a fiery napalm concoction housed in a 500lb shell. The munitions of death were the daily specials served up by the battleship New Jersey. The seafood special, high in the sky brought in by the B52s. Oh how that serving cratered as a 500lb bomb hit the earth, digging deep and crushing the underground hospitals and hiding places of the VC and NVA. For the smokers, we can smoke in this restaurant! We had Puff the Dragon ship coming in with Gatling guns, each firing 6000 rounds per minute laced with tracer rounds to find its customers.

The smorgasbord of mayhem and death is a franchise blueprinted and designed and will cater anywhere in the world and are implemented by those high on the food chain. The dynamics of war must have these added ingredients that will confuse can cause a dizzying effect. Wars come with clever schemes, plots and subplots, hidden agendas, everyone along with an open agenda so that the hidden agenda gets little attention.

On any given day, Vietnam had 378 covert missions in play. I don't know the exact numbers, but I can tell you firsthand, I observed teams of CIA operatives operating in the villages from time to time. The CIA was financed by the black marketing schemes of drugs, cigarettes, coca cola, booze or anything else of value. I remember a time one of their sales reps, a young Vietnamese girl, was offering me a carton of cigarettes for $10. I thought, since I'm packing heat, I'll just takes the cigarettes, put my M16 in her face and say "Sorry Charlie", which was what I did. Word eventually got back that I had stepped on the wrong toes. These cigarettes were owned and distributed by the CIA. So, the simple way to put it is, she eventually got her $10. It just wasn't worth it. That was one of the many ways I came into contact with the CIA. They carried out assassinations and changing whatever they saw fit to change or their needs. This was going on all over Vietnam, in order to try to turn the tide of the war since back in the states the American people were fed up. A lot of people who were eager to do anything, well, who was going to stop them? These little people called the VC and NVA were doing pretty good when they were outgunned. It's amazing the views out of context when examining the Vietnam War. My view and my credentials to voice are twofold experience. Whoever coined the term "Hindsight is 20/20", the war as whole in Vietnam was a lie. This fact and truth opens up clever schemes and misdirection plays so the mainstream can follow the obvious and what gives the appearance of doing good and right for the poor and crushed Vietnam people.

Below the surface, just a little bit is where you'll find the treasure and real deal. Vietnam hatched more plots and subplots almost equal God's church today. There are more betrayals, coup d'états, regime changes, driven by a spirit of competition and weak people of God who won't get their own anointing and marching orders. I must say there are sectors and pockets of good going on, just like in Vietnam. The enemies at work in Vietnam knew how to divide and conquer. The spirits of division are alive and well, and it's very clear that a regime or country, a house divided cannot stand.

The big difference between a splintered regime and God's army is, God will have his way and God is more than enough to complete his plan. There is no God like my God.

A LETTER FROM A SON

Hey Dad,

I just wanted to take a moment and reflect on what this day means to me, and the twist that it has on my life as well as yours.

Veteran's Day is a celebration of Veterans past and present. It also reminds me of an 18 year old boy forced to be a man and do inhuman things to other people, and to not be human for a time or else your life would be taken as well. I look back at a time where our country hated itself and its boys who were fighting to spread freedom like our boys now. But they had little or no support from the home front. I see a generation of lost men, trying to this very day to be accepted and appreciated for fighting a controversial war, in which they did their duty as Americans when called upon. I take classes because I am bettering my future – all because you gave up your college years, your innocence and your health to fight for a country that didn't love you.

I have a great memory of thoughts and feelings I have had over the years. I can remember sitting with you in the mornings while you would get ready for work, and thinking now neat it was to watch you shave and get ready to put food in your family's mouths. I remember long drives to Bedford and talking your ear off. I can think of times where you and I have talked and my thoughts during those conversations. What bothers me is seeing an 18 year old boy alone in the jungle and trying to picture what you were thinking. The mindset for you at the time must have been terrible, and I know you can still put yourself there and remember the things racing through your mind. Seeing yourself sick and your body deteriorating with Agent Orange must trigger those thoughts.

I'll never get sick of hearing about that war and my fascination with it. Every day you get up and cough, you are reminded of what you were doing/thinking at 18 years old. Every day that I am in school and I think about my well being, it's because an 18 year old boy used his head right and didn't lose his life. Because of these small things and a day like veteran's Day, we are all reminded of something. While the WW2 veterans get all the praise for accomplishing winning the last Great War, I believe all Vietnam Veterans should receive the same praise for fighting as individuals. Our country didn't back all of you, making it the toughest war we'll ever know. I have no doubt the years of your life have been cut short for the hell you endured.

That's why on this day, I want you to think about your mindset at 18 (as hard as it may be) and be thankful that you made all the choices that you've made. Even the bad ones have created something. I don't want you to have any regrets for the terrible things you have done. Because of what you did, I am sitting at school typing this email.

Steven R. Mitchell

November 11, 2004

PERSPECTIVE FROM THE VIETNAMESE PEOPLE

I think that in any war, you've got to gain a good perspective of the people. Not so much the ones fighting, but the people that were basically right in the middle of an ongoing war. They didn't have a voice because Vietnam was split into so many factions. The North trying to push their will on the South. The fracture of the Viet Cong, which were all related to the people throughout the country. These were those who were against the South Vietnamese government and had aligned themselves with the North. So you have all these dynamics in play. Most of the South Vietnamese people were unarmed.

My assignments were in Laos, Cambodia, North Vietnam and the DMZ. I had many different assignments in the Northern sector. When we were introduced to the people in Quang Tri village, we were a well armed, high combat force of American Marines. They threw us together with these people under the Pacification program. Put it this way, they were not used to seeing us. We'd never interacted with Vietnamese people to begin with. We were out in the bush most of the time and we just killed anyone who looked like them, since they looked like the enemy. It was hard to separate in split second timing in a fluid war. When you mix all this together without any knowledge of who these people really are, it's a recipe for disaster and not fair to the Vietnamese people. We weren't ready. It was the wrong fit for us to have anything to do with the people, Pacification or the ARVNs we had to train. It was a ticking timebomb. It was not well thought out by the brass or the politicians or whoever was putting the plans together.

One of the other fundamental factors that seemed to be a missing piece to the mix was the religious beliefs of the people - which we had no knowledge of.

Mainly my men and I looked at everyone as VC. We killed some VC in the bush. We knew a little about them, but our fight was mainly with the NVA. These people resembled the VC. From their perspective, keep in mind as you boil it down simply, their main concern wasn't the politics of Vietnam. Their priority was, "Will I have a bowl of rice today?"

In the village we operated out of (Quang Tri) this was some of the poorest conditions you can imagine. They had rice paddies, water bulls for work, a big black cast iron pot for rice cooking and a few utensils. But that's about it. The hooches were grass topped mixed with whatever they could piece together. Very simple living conditions. This was their home, where they raised their families.

You could multiply this scene throughout Vietnam. The biggest thing was rice and fishing. These were the "crops" that kept everyone alive. Not much else. They had to deal with the idea that they worked hard, and at any time the VC would come into their village and take what they wanted. If they needed rice, they took it. These Vietnamese people were constantly at the mercy of whoever had the AK47 or the M16. That was their life. So they just looked at us as someone else with weapons. They didn't want us there. We were interrupting their life. A simple life, but theirs. And we were messing it up. When we hit their village, it turned their world upside down.

So as we entered the village, it was total chaos. My men and I were out of control. They were out of control. My job was to train 100 ARVN troops in combat, ambushes, tactics and the like. Their colonel was under my command. His troops were not trained to read maps or a compass. They had no idea on much of anything. I'm not sure what they did all day, to be honest. So there were clashes constantly. I had my orders and didn't like any of them. These people didn't have much of anything, and what they did have, they just wanted to be left alone. They just wanted to pursue their religion without any outside interference. it wasn't the villagers saying they wanted change. Change would come slowly. It didn't need to be forced onto them by war. The French were there before and they lost. Before the French were the Chinese and they lost too. Then we came in. Decades of the same thing. We napalmed their land. We brought Agent Orange. We dropped 500 pound bombs on them. We killed and wounded many in the name of "collateral damage". Mistakes all the way around.

Agent Orange has devastated their land. For 10,000 years, this toxic stew won't allow anything to grow. The dioxons and poisons have caused deformities, diseases and cancers. The US is still awarding benefits and money for anything tied to Agent Orange. Just a small amount of Agent Orange is devastating. I know its taken a huge toll on the American Veteran. It's an invisible enemy that's still attacking the Vietnamese people too. I've seen pictures of severe deformities in Vietnamese children due to it. Hospitals have filled up with related problems and diseases. The mines and booby traps over there are still maiming the people as well. So the war lives on today.

Years later as my view changes, I think how crazy was that for them? Imagine the hometown you live in. Suddenly armed soldiers from another country come down the street and tell you what to do. They didn't know Americans. From the time I was in Vietnam, I know that we tried different tactics with the people. Some of the operations involved relocating entire villages located in hot spots. Sometimes they were just too intertwined with the VC. So theses people had to be totally relocated to a new place. Everything was completely relocated either by truck or chopper. This had to be a devastating blow! They were being dictated to by foreigners. it just wasn't fair.

Another thing I remember was, the Americans came in and killed anyone who was of VC age. We killed everyone 16-17-18, we just killed them all to eradicate them. This came out much later in the war, but were some of the strategies. You'd go into area that were VC strongholds and the order was to execute all who were VC, which they did.

We didn't respect any of their religion either. I had no idea about Buddha or their pagoda temples. Immediately, we just went in and blew them up, infuriating the people. Relate that today with the Muslims. If you were to draw a cartoon of Mohammed, they would go insane. So you can imagine the reaction when we desecrated their temples. But we were not indoctrinated to any of it. Up to that point, our missions had been Search and Destroy. We hunted and sought out the enemy. That's all we did. Now our new job is to pacify village people? It was insane. Why would you send in hard core killer Marines to a village of South Vietnamese people and expect them to be cool, calm and collected? Fact is, these people were definitely sympathetic to the VC. They looked at us as temporary, but the VC would be there long after we were gone. They would definitely come back. They were always very close as well. There could be payback when we leave.

The thing I didn't know, which was yet another insane piece was, the ARVN troops were actually VC. Not sympathetic, they WERE VC. We had no way of recognizing or discerning that. It only came through a later event. The bottom line was, the ones making the orders at the top had no idea what they were doing. So they threw a bunch of people together and it didn't turn out real well. It's turning out the same way in Iraq and Afghanistan, and it all boils down to their religious beliefs. The Shiites and the Sunnis are fighting the same religious war that the North and South Vietnamese were. The same thing happened in Bosnia between the Croats and the Serbs. It was all about religion. What have we learned through all this? The enemy is smart. We're only going to be there a short amount of time. The people are going to get tired of the war and yank the military out. Then all the blood, hurt, deaths and sacrifices will be just a hollow, victory. You'd have to be there for the next century to turn that around. In Vietnam, the enemy would flee to Cambodia. Now in Afghanistan, they flee to Pakistan.

I think it's important to remember that war is not just black and white or good and bad. There is good and evil on both sides. We did our wrongs there in Vietnam and bit off more than we could chew at times. The consensus is, it was a mistake to go. 58,000+ dead and 300,000+ wounded and more dying every day. It was a mistake. From a war perspective, we haven't learned our lessons. We're in two different types of Vietnam now and there won't be a victory. Our will and the American people is strained and weak. They won't stand for it much longer, especially now in these economic troubles. There will not be a victory. We'll be somewhere else in no time at all, but the same scenario will play over and over again.

You've got to assess the cost of war and post war. Without a major victory in Iraq or Afghanistan, it's just Vietnam repeating itself.

The fact is, no one has learned a thing.

"THERE'S NOTHING MORE WE CAN DO TO HELP STEVE"

Those were the last words spoken to me and my wife by my VA psychologist, Dr. David Pfenninger as he sat crying at our last session. Up in arms over months and months of trying to treat my PTSD, he threw in the towel. With tears streaming down his face, he explained that they had done all they could do to help me, and they were finished. He recommended I never go to a VA hospital again. Shortly after leaving the PTSD program at the VA, the Head of Psychiatry there committed suicide. So how were they supposed to help me?

I'd spent several years in and out of VA hospitals and there really was nothing they could do for me. I was angry about the war. I was angry for them not taking care of us all like they'd promised. I was angry at them for denying my claim when they had a pill bottle with my name and serial number right on it. I was angry. And I made sure they all knew it. In this chapter, I'm going to lay out a few excerpts of the "world's words" about me.

From my Friend, Rick Thompson – October 5, 1990

"The Steve Mitchell I knew before he went into the Marines and over to Vietnam is not the same Steve Mitchell I knew when he returned....he came back angry and full of hate for our government. He was no longer that...full of life person...but rather was a withdrawn observer. Steve would get periodic fits of rage and would do bodily harm to anyone who would get in his way...It was frightening and explosive rage. Steve and I were roommates...upon his return from Vietnam. There were many nights he would be in his room fast asleep and then begin screaming and breaking out in a sweat...Are there behavioral changes in Steve since his tour in Vietnam? You bet there are, and not one of them can we as a country be proud of."

Steven M. Herman, PhD – Department of Veterans Affairs – March 30, 1994

"Mr. Steven Mitchell exhibits numerous symptoms of PTSD, including recurrent and intrusive thoughts, nightmares and flashbacks...he manifests significant symptoms of emotional and cognitive avoidance...detachment and estrangement from others...he additionally manifests sleep problems, significant levels of irritability and anger discontrol...and exaggerated startle response...

David Pfenninger, PhD –Department of Veterans Affairs – April 19, 1994

"Mr. Mitchell suffers from a severe variant of combat related Post Traumatic Stress Disorder stemming directly from his tour in Vietnam…In addition to these Post Traumatic Stress Disorder symptoms, he also has respiratory and skin problems which are due to toxic agents and anti-foliants also incurred during his Vietnam service…The net result is…he is a quite debilitated man at present and will require ongoing intensive therapies to help him learn to manage…it is extremely unlikely that this man will be able to return to gainful employment in the competitive labor market in the near future."

David Pfenninger, PhD –Department of Veterans Affairs – June 6, 1994

"Mr. Mitchell was deeply traumatized at the time of his Vietnam combat service and that the onset of post Traumatic Stress Disorder was immediate, severe and enduring. This has represented a severe disabling condition for him; making it virtually impossible for him to maintain employment…It has also had adverse effects on his relationship with family, friends and culture at large."

Steven M. Herman, PhD – Department of Veterans Affairs – July 28, 1994

"Mr. Mitchell has been hospitalized twice this calendar year for his PTSD symptomatology. It is clear that he will be needing ongoing treatment to assist him further in his recovery, as that road has been made more difficult by his pervasive sense of identity confusion, and his tendency to push people away. It is my hope…to see Mr.

Mitchell…be able to move on with his life. At this point, however, that day is not yet visible."

One thing we should keep at the forefront of our minds at all times is, "God will always have the final say." His word will not return void. He is the Alpha and Omega; the beginning and the end. His Word is a living word, and he makes the final decision concerning my life and yours. I could easily take these words spoken to me and written about me and let them take root in my heart and spirit. But that would not be the right decision. Instead, I've decided to take the words God has spoken about me – both to me directly and through others – and allow those words to shape me and mold me, like the potter's clay that I am.

Jeremiah 18:1-10

*"This is the word that came to Jeremiah from the LORD: "Go down to the potter's house, and there I will give you my message." So I went down to the potter's house, and I saw him working at the wheel. But the pot he was shaping from the clay was marred in his hands; so the potter formed it into another pot, shaping it as seemed best to him. Then the word of the LORD came to me. He said, "Can I not do with you, Israel, as this potter does?" declares the LORD. "**Like clay in the hand of the potter, so are you in my hand**, Israel. If at any time I announce that a nation or kingdom is to be uprooted, torn down and destroyed, and if that nation I warned repents of its evil, then I will relent and not inflict on it the disaster I had planned. And if at another time I announce that a nation or kingdom is to be built up and planted, and if it does evil in my sight and does not obey me, then I will reconsider the good I had intended to do for it."*

GOD SAYS....

I'll minister to you from the depths of my soul.
Let me see your comfort with the love I bestow.
Lord I want to serve you from the table of my heart,
To fill you with adoration for your gift of a new start.
I'll minister to you. I'll minister to you. I'll minister to you.

-A song by Jackie Mitchell – 5/4/09

Isn't that powerful? To think, when the world says what it says, we can rely on our Heavenly Father to minister to us. No matter where we are, who we are, what we think we've become or why we are where we are, HE will come to minister. Think about that for a moment.

So I have compiled a few of the things God has said to me through others. I place these here to remind myself and to show you that God has the final say, and it is not over until the Lord of Hosts says it is!

"He was in a war he couldn't win. It was designed to lose. He cannot trust authority because when something goes wrong or the orders don't seem to be toward victory, he thinks he is going to lose

again. So he won't follow orders…I have designed the battle to win but he won't get in the war…Tell him to get into the war, that I will guarantee victory. I will not betray him. I will lead him to the victory."

Through Jackie Mitchell – 4/2000

"Do not be discouraged or dismayed. Our War Chief is giving us strategy for weapons of our warfare…The weapons he gives us must first be effective in our own personal lives…then you can use that weapon effectively. It may take some time to see a battle through, but you will see VICTORY. Keep lookin' up Man of God. Our redemption draweth nigh. Joshua 1:5-9 is for you, General…And my prayer for you is to be effective, thorough and complete in your walk and in all you do for him."

Through Sam Hicks – 6/2000

"God was showing me that the Captain of the Lord of Hosts has come and hovered over both of you…You are both soldiers in his Army. Not only just a soldier but of the highest rank…God is saying by the prophetic…You're going to destroy the works of the enemy, that the strongholds are going to fall down…You are going to return to that country where you were with those people in war and God is going to use you to bring Christ into that nation…the power of God is going to be on both of you."

Through Pastor Patsy – 4/1997

"Steve, I saw you as a masterpiece tapestry. God is tying up the loose ends. The frayed ends are being healed up. God is weaving you tightly with him…The end result will be a beautiful tapestry of God's

handiwork and will see your life as an inspiration. Jackie, I felt God broke a spirit of heaviness, grief and sorrow. A new season of rejoicing. Wells the enemy has clogged and stopped are opened up. You'll write songs from this season and minister hope to the hurting."

Through Karla – 2001

"You can't teach others what you haven't learned. But through your experiences or trials, you will cause victory to others because you overcome. Through all of this…your anointing grows and prospers. Move into your appointed time and destiny. Saddle up and move out!"

Through Jackie Mitchell

"I saw you in a foxhole with the Lord, and you were looking through binoculars. You turned to the Lord and said, 'I see it, they're coming'. The Lord smiled and nodded yes. The lord then said you would be sent out to tell what was coming.

Through Jackie Mitchell

"I heard 'Our God is a God of deliverances and surely he shall shatter the head of the enemy'. That is what the Lord is going to do for you…He's already begun that work."

Through Pastor Diane Engler – 4/1997

"You have the kind of heart God has…People are scared of you because of your background, but…You've got God's heart. Buddy, you're gonna touch the hurtin' like nobody has ever touched the hurtin'. You're gonna stand for God like nobody has stood for God, because your heart is right. Even the commendation you got from the

service, that wasn't because of bravery. That was because of your heart. As soon as that old war deal is finished…this man's gonna change things around you."

Through Pastor Frank Seebransingh – 8/1997

"I will train you to fight with truth, with your love for others and with my ways. Take hold of every situation to expel the enemy and claim the land. Use my words from your mouth as weapons of victory instead of bringing defeat. Use the grace that was given to you to rescue others for my kingdom."

Through Jackie Mitchell – 8/2005

"The days of weeping are over, for the sorrows are gone…Yes, you will speak to the wounded hearts. You will do it through the power of my Holy Spirit.

Through Mike Bournique – 4/1997

"Don't be like Saul; anointed, but he never used it for the right purposes. He let his anger and his fleshly desires dictate his destiny…God says you've been a rebel without a cause. Now, you're a rebel with a cause for the Kingdom of God. You haven't been fightin' flesh and blood, buddy. You've been fightin' the old demons of the past. Now I want you to give your emotions to God…God's not done yet."

Through Kevin Leal – 3/1995

WHY IS THIS TRUCK ON MY CHEST?

Just when you think you've got it all figured out – your destiny, your sonship, being sent out into ministry – you get stopped. First let me say, "It ain't over til it's over", and that's only when God says so regarding all things. I thought, "Hey, I'm a good son. The timing is right." Everything seemed lined up and I was ready to go, ready for the fight and the war. I felt as if I'd been in the trenches for years, fighting and training. I was anointed for battle in my eyes, but God sees things so differently sometimes. I was ready to stretch and take the leap of faith, and I felt like so many other soldiers in the natural who are so trained and equipped for battle. Most will cry out, "Give me a mission". I thought I was ready to take ground, take no prisoners and fulfill my destiny by doing what I was born to do. It's forward ho, but God says "No". Now I've got to regroup when I thought I was on the launch pad. However, it's not about me or you, it's about the one who called us and set us free. God has done so much for me that my attitude is to represent him well. So many times in the past I would disqualify myself from ministry positions and teaching/leadership roles because I knew I wasn't ready. I had unfinished business.

Now, I know God will never leave me or forsake me, but have you ever felt like you and the Lord were playing hide and seek? We must seek him and knock down the door. As we pray and pursue, he will be found. The enemy plays with our minds and emotions. He lies, gets us to question everything about our relationship with God and our calling and destiny. We have to renew our minds daily with the Word to counteract his lies and deceptions. We know we are not forsaken, yet we feel alone. We are loved by our Heavenly Father, yet we feel rejected at times. This must be overcome, we all know that. My road of preparation has been a long one, but I know that I have purpose and a mission to fulfill for my Lord. Yet this present situation I found myself in was so unexpected.

I had been walking the track at our local high school when I began to have severe leg pain. I promptly began paying for healing and relief. It would subside until the next time I walked, and then it would return. I walked through it and didn't think that there might be a problem, which is not always the best response as I would soon learn. Two weeks went by and as I was walking the pain went to my chest – hence the "Truck on my chest". I barely made it to my car as I was out of breath and in quite a bit of pain. I made it home and asked my wife to pray for me. She was not at peace with the situation and called the doctor. When his office told us they could not see us until late that afternoon, we decided to be cautious and go to the emergency room. Good idea! I was promptly admitted, and the next morning taken into surgery to unblock two arteries. The third needed to be treated with medication before unblocking it. My wife had to force me to go – force me to listen to the doctor's orders, and even told the nurse I was a flight risk and should be cuffed to the bed! I am definitely a bad patient, but sometimes being flat on your back gives you the best perspective to hear and listen. I asked myself, "Why did this happen? What can I learn from it?" First come the lies through the voice of the enemy, telling me I was never called. I had made it up in my own mind. He threw a dozen other untruths to mess with my mind. Now, this stage can take as long as you allow it to consume you. Satan can only operate as long as you allow him. So stop as fast as possible and get your head and heart into God's word. I gave these lies a moment, but quickly came to myself, knowing that God was the map maker of my lfe and destiny, and I was definitely called with a purpose. Still, I am flat on my back in a hospital bed trying to learn something. Well, ask and you shall receive! My heart was ready. I wanted answers and God was talking.

Since the jungles of Vietnam, where I was surrounded by death, I carried with me what professional psychiatrists call "Survivor's Guilt". It is a demonic attachment that is one of the many parts of Post Traumatic Stress Disorder (PTSD). You may live and make it out of the horrors of war, but you are still a casualty at another time and place. The forces of darkness never let you forget. Satan loves to rewind pictures in your mind and torment you for being alive. The battle in the natural may be over, but the spiritual battle continues to rage on. The spiritual enemies never want you to have peace, and are threatened by the survivor because of his testimony. Without realizing it, I had confessed that I had died in Vietnam. I had carried and bagged enough of my comrades that I had begun to feel dead inside. In some eerie sort of way, this somehow eases the pain of surviving. My actions after coming home were always severe – to snumb the pain from the mental torment. I would take drugs by the handful instead of one or two. Even my buddies would try to warn me of this danger. I would always respond that I wanted to blow my heart out. The scene was repeated over and over again, but thanks to God, he never allowed me to die.

I realized that I had never dealt with this problem. I'm a burier. I dig deep and think this will help me. But God is a digger too, and he wants to uncover those things that hinder us. When I first started my walking program, I used it to de-stress, thinking this was a good relief from mental warfare. It was just another hiding place, after all. I first began having problems with my left ankle. The pain was off the charts. I must have looked like an idiot, dragging this leg along as I was walking. I was thinking, "No pain, no gain!" As I got to the last laps of my walk, the pain would subside. I thought I was overcoming something. We had a prayer meeting once a week in our home, and we lifted up the need for healing in my ankle. The feedback was awesome. My wife, Jackie had a vision of Jesus standing behind me, and he kissed me on the head. He was staying with me. I was confident that all was well, so in the morning I headed for the track to walk again. My thoughts were of healing and a green light for ministry to begin. I couldn't wait to test my ankle and shout victory. After less than one lap, I knew I had a bigger problem. It felt like a truck had landed on my chest. My biggest challenge now was to see if I could make it to the car and get home. My vision blurred, my mouth was dry and my mind was racing with thoughts of yesterday's prayer meeting. I was asking the entire why, how and what questions on this kamikaze drive into negative thinking. It wasn't until after the surgery that God began to answer me and reveal to me that I still had the wrong thinking. Since the war, I had lived without care of death or what I was doing to those who loved me. I was angry at myself for surviving, thinking I had done something wrong while the dead had done something right. My thinking had hurt me and my family, and God wanted it to stop. I hadn't taken care of myself or my twisted thinking. I hadn't ever cared. I was so wrong! In addition to my physical experience, my emergency room meeting with God had begun.

God is the true heart specialist. He is the revealer of truth and the healing for us in body, mind, spirit and soul. God showed me that my life was NOT my life, but in fact, his. I had played around with medications, wrong eating habits and carried a death wish. I was always doing it my way, but that is no way to live. It's the way to die without fulfillment of the course for God. My path has now been corrected. My body and mind has once again been healed by a true loving Father and Savior.

Once again, I continue to press toward the mark of the high calling....

Isaiah 55:7-9

Let the wicked forsake his way, and the unrighteous man his thoughts: and let him return unto the LORD, and he will have mercy upon him; and to our God, for he will abundantly pardon.

For my thoughts are not your thoughts, neither are your ways my ways, saith the LORD.

For as the heavens are higher than the earth, so are my ways higher than your ways, and my thoughts than your thoughts.

C.U.E. CASE

C.U.E, stands for "clear and unmistakable error". I also like to call it the "WBH factor", which stands for "We've Been Had".

The Vulture Assassins (the VA) are trained and operate in a world of beaureaucratic red tape. The rules and legal standards are as sure as the Deepwater Horizon oil rig in the Gulf of Mexico. The language of the Vulture Assassin is foreign to anything you can encounter. It's the language of liars and thieves that can distort a disability claim that is beyond any reasonable doubt. But predictability ends up in their favor.

A good example was when I was going through the process of my Cue case after decades of fighting a corrupt and broken Vulture Assassin system. The year was 2009 and I'm 40 years into my cue case. The Vulture Assassins dig up a relic of a doctor who's name was Dr Noble - who was probably activated in World War 1. In 2009 this so-called Doctor had to be brought out of a long retirement. The thing that stood out most was not only was he beyond retirement and blind - as he had trouble focusing with his Hubbell-grade glasses - prior to seeing this Boxie, (which is medic in Vietnamese) I was put through a series of WBH appointments.

I went before Judge Lisa Bernard who at the end of the hearing that she would open my C File and examine each piece of evidence - all support claims. Over 40 years of hard evidence, testimony, writing senators and Congressmen and heads of VA, and veteran's advocates with a backbone to stand up to these Vulture Assassin. The more than enough evidence awaited Judge Bernard, but somehow her bold statement was empty, The WBH factor was still alive and well. Oh it gets better!

Another WBH episode was in 2007, and this gem will hit the Vulture Assassin reruns as the Vulture Culture hits new lows. In 2007, 40 years into my case, I went to my local Vulture Assassin clinic in Fort Myers Florida for emergency treatment, as my skin disease was off the charts. The infected area covered 60-80 percent of my body. The bleeding and the swelling needed something new because after 40 years of treating this out of control disease from the jungles of Vietnam, I was immune to about everything. I had to be careful what medications to take, because of the effect on my liver and kidneys. The medications like grifalvin and grizactin had taken their toll after treatment.

The Vulture Assassins hatched a brilliant plan, and that was to call me back and take pictures of the infected area. Wow. After 40 years why not? It's a date with the Vulture Assassin's photographer. We were just getting warned up in the photo shoot, and I just couldn't get comfortable with the Vulture Assassin photographer. As close-up shots are taken now, here's where the photo shoot goes bad. We get some real winners of my arms and legs and the Vulture Assassin wants to pull the plug on the shoot! Wait a minute, not so fast! There's more! My chest and back hasn't been taken. And the response was, "That's enough." You guessed it, the WBH is all over this shoot. I'm just getting comfortable and relaxed after each pose, and now I'm no longer popular. The best analogy for this WBH photo shoot would be a detective on a crime scene. A murder has taken place and on the ground is a smoking gun. The detective declares, "That's it, I've got enough", leaving the smoking gun. This should open up your eyes and understanding to the obvious corrupt tactics of these Vulture Assassins. Let's not acquire all the evidence.

Another recent step in the WBH series, was going before a DRO, or review officer in 2010. Does any of this make you dizzy? This DRO was given the same script as Judge Bernard. To get the real effects of this, as you read this book read it out loud slow and bassy at 33 1/2 rpms the following:

"I will take your case and examine each document - all evidence piece by piece, in your C File"

Both the DRO and Judge Lisa Bernard are equal actors and both applied the same effort, which was none. Each time the stinging effects of WBH are loud and clear.

Now, it's time to finish with old Dr. Noble (who even smelled old). Dr Noble's assignment was to examine me, providing that his heart continued beating. Prior to entering his office I brought along my attorney, David C. Cory, because simply these Vulture Assassins engage in lying, cheating and stealing from Freedom Fighters. We had a situation where these Vulture Assassins didn't like the idea that my attorney was present, and wanted to join the good doctor and myself. Seems simple. But you must remember, these Vulture Assassins operate in the shadows - basically back shooters if you know what I mean. After a major fight, my attorney was denied access when my permission was given. Would you be surprised if I told you Dr. Noble knew nothing about my case?

We came armed with my complete C File. To pull evidence and pictures and medical evidence. That's not how the Vulture Assassins operate! In the end I was granted service connection back to 1972, but with no rating.

Ow! Ow! Ow! Can you feel the WBH?

I'm covered up to 80% of my body and there's no rating.

There is a special place in hell for these Vulture Assassins and Dr. Noble needs to repent before he takes his last breath.

WE'VE BEEN HAD– THE VA

One learns quickly the war does not wind down, but heats up quickly in the vast jungle of your soul. It is waiting to inflict a new toll as the reality of war holds steady. The first reality that hits and doesn't seem real is the many voices shouting, "You've made it! You've made it!" The constant answer is, "Made what?" These two words never make it out though, as you try to figure out why you're disappointed. This launches an intense battle in my soul as I desperately try to walk through a new door and into a new chapter in my life. I don't have the strength or know how to get there, because I am a prisoner of the past. I am chained to the war zone they said I made it out of. This is living hell, and a sentence that many of us received.

The shock and awe of the Vietnam War hit us when we rotated back to the world. We had to face a new adversary from within. This new enemy popped up from a well concealed vantage point, like an assassin, hungry to deliver their pain and death. The very VA culture that was set up to assist freedom fighters has turned to feast on them like vultures hungry for meat. This time these predators are feasting on war-torn patriots that have come home already ravaged by war and very few of them have the energy left for these kind of serious war games. I speak first about those who have engaged in high combat, worn down by the effects of operating in jungle conditions, that includes extreme heat beyond anything we've experienced in the states. I'm talking about heat that kills. I've seen many drop from heat exhaustion, and some even drop dead.

The distribution of C Rations should have killed many of us, especially the pork steak. I used C4 to cook the pork steak and I still ended up throwing it away. To further drive this point home, someone out there in the bush, a Marine who was always think about ways to kill, showed us a brilliant method to serve up our enemies' food poisoning that kills and hopefully causes a violent and slow death. This sneaky death chow, depending on how we punctured the pork steak can, was placed in the bush like this lovely meal that just fell out of a backpack. This method was popular, because I never came across a Marine that liked pork steak. I like to get off pork steak, but just one more point – our squad was operating in Quang Tri village, engaged in the famous Pacification program.

We were stuck there during the monsoon rains, and were desperate for food, so even rat was preferred above pork steak. My final thoughts are – shame on you whatever American meat company that sold pork steak to the US Government. I know your profit margin was obscene and you obviously had no conscience. It had to come from sickened, diseased pigs, maybe even road kill lying in the hot sun for days. The only good use for pork steak was we served it to our enemies in a sneaky way.

In the Nam and deep in the jungle, an array of bugs and insects covered the terrain and ruled their sector with their own battle raging. Our main concern was with the death flyers – the mosquitoes – that seemed to drive you insane when you first arrived. We were introduced to these mosquitoes that would dive bomb and suck loads of blood day or night. Night time was the worst. We fought back with repellant, however I found that what works best was being out in the bush for long durations without a shower. This thick crust of sweat and dirt created a protective barrier that at least made it bearable, as the mosquitoes were always with us. Snakes and other jungle varmints staged their own attacks when the opportunities were there. The bamboo viper was always one to look for because, just like our enemy, it was small and deadly.

The Vietnam War provided a series of battles and firefights, each one different than the next. The human waves of suicide volunteers and non volunteers took its toll. The incoming rounds and ambushes left you numb and traumatized, which is jungle norm. The trauma of war and the wounds deep in your mind like were someone taking a hammer, inflicting blow after blow, some deeper and costlier than others, but each hitting the mark. What's left if the jungle fighter lives, is anyone's guess and must be played out in real time. Whoever you were before will never be realized again, nor can ever be recaptured to its original painting. Now you're a walking, breathing fake in a sense that your identity doesn't fit anymore. Many of us found that we were now strangers in our own land, our own sectors, our own families and our own bodies.

What was can never be again. Most of the memories are gone with only fragments left. My childhood memories, growing up, Mom and Dad, siblings and friends had changed now, and not for the better. Their son and brother was completely changed and not the makeover anyone would want. I can best be described as a walking bomb, ready to explode and deliver pain and death, while at the same time desiring a peaceful transition that was never going to happen.

My parents knew that something huge was very different about the Steve they once knew. A big eye-opener was when I sent them pictures of me eating my lunch on a pile of dead bodies, stacked after human waves hit our perimeter. My parents escaped to a place called denial. My brothers and sister at the time thought everything would be back to normal in no time. Obviously that was not to be. The silence of being back in the world was eerie but should have been welcomed. However the sounds of war would return in my mind as I would revisit each instrument of war like a symphony and the full sound of an orchestra. The high notes of rockets and mortars in the air before impact. The bass cracking from an AK47, to deep rumbling sounds of 500lb bombs as they crater deep into Charlie's hideaways and underground hospitals.

Going deep into isolation seemed to be the recipe for Vietnam veterans. To mingle outside our hole always seemed to be trouble. We were like a gunfighter from the Old West who was desperately trying to change and settle down from enemies that always seemed to come in a never-ending stream. It seemed that it took more effort to lay down the violent past, full of tales of life and death scenarios, with each one carrying different outcomes and costs. The wages of war has its cost in ways that cannot be easily measured. Each war crime has its own price, and its intrinsic value is tied to that particular trauma of war. For me, shooting a sapper boy in the face at close range – one who was 8-12 years old – caused me buckets of blood type grief. The psychological snapping sound from this event cost me years of trying to escape through heavy doses of drugs, violence and alcohol - anything that could numb me if for only a few seconds. The chase of many war vets ends for some in death or prison, or cutting this path over and over again. This cycle takes you into a black hole where closure can only be found with forgiveness from Jesus Christ.

The WBH factor comes out of nowhere and nobody is expecting it. Nothing can prepare a war torn veteran coming home from hell in the late 60s and mid 70s, when we made our final exit that I can find the words for. The promise of war from our government is this: If something happens to you as a solider fighting for your country in a war zone, the other side of the contract is "we will take care of your needs and all that entails". All service connected injuries will be treated by every means possible and the government will compensate on a fair and honest basis. The promise is actually broader than the specifics mentioned, but I will keep it simple. The WBH factor hits each of us differently, because of the vultures and assassins that operate freelance with the full support of this broken and corrupt culture called the VA System. Talk about weapons of mass destruction!

The VA system and culture was set up to assist veterans from war to civilian life. From the early 60s to the mid 70s, our government and the American taxpayers made a huge commitment to the war in Vietnam. The meter began running as soon as we sent in advisors. Soon after, we sent waves after wave of soldiers from all walks of life. The costs of the war are still being measured. The meter for the casualties of war is still running. We can continue to build more walls, but the wall I would like to see built is one named WBH - We've Been Had.

The Gulf War vets can build their own war, as they've been had too. The eye opener for these patriots is called Gulf War Syndrome. The word "Syndrome" seems much more evasive. It seems much more invisible, but it is very real to those warriors who now seek help from those vultures and assassins. The vultures of this broken VA system prey on the unsuspecting war torn vet. These vultures feed on and take advantage of the wounded warrior at a critical time. The assassin nature of this culture is demonstrated over and over, as they strike by surprise and slowly drain whatever fight the war vet has left. He now has to use whatever energy and means available to take on a government and bureaucracy who seem to enjoy taking advantage of these vets who are not armed any longer. They have little knowledge of the rules of engagement or language of their new enemy. The payment of these vultures and assassins comes in the form of their government pay and bonus system, as they steal from the very freedom fighters who have already given so much. Now they have to fight again in an arena that is fixed and the house wins in most cases. In this case, the house is the government.

Because the commitment to the Vietnam War began back in the 60s, by the time we hit the mid 70s, the government hit both the OS button and the DS button, neither of which I should need to explain to a Veteran reading this! Both buttons represent dollars, or post war costs. These buttons are being hit again as we examine the costs, starting with Gulf War Syndrome. OS and DS buttons means make ready the vultures and assassins and let them feast and strike at the very core of America. The American soldier deserves more than this. The American families represented in all these wars deserve better. It's time to dismantle this broken and corrupt VA system, which many times cheats the veteran with an honest and legitimate case. Many vultures and assassins of the VA chose to engage in lying to and cheating a veteran rather than do the right and just thing.

I have fought the Vulture Assassins for over 42 years. I have what's called a C.U.E. case - a clear and unmistakable error case. In short, in 1969 after almost 13 months in the jungle, I went from Vietnam to a hospital in Yokosuka, Japan. I arrived at Yokosuka Naval Hospital, where I was assigned a Navy doctor, Dr. Snodgrass to be treated for my broken hand and a sever skin disease that covered most of my body.

I remember our first encounter with Agent Orange. It was as exciting as being introduced to a new weapon ,or watching Puff operate for the first time and light up the sky with tracer rounds as it lays down a lethal dose, hitting each grid. We set up our perimeter and were briefed on a plane coming in with a load of jungle killer. We didn't know what to expect, but what we did know that Agent Orange was supposed to kill the jungle immediately. So when we were on patrol the next day, Charlie wouldn't be able to hide. The plane came in as planned, unloading the chemicals, banking left and right like a crop duster. Only this cargo was more potent, as the jungle began to crack and pop as though it was trying to vomit out the harmful toxic stew that was killing it. The jungle knew what we didn't – that Agent Orange was killing everything, including us.

The wind carried the deadly mist into our position, and it stung as the Agent Orange entered our system through the open cuts on our bodies caused by cutting through this thick jungle. This setting was close to river crossing where we filled our canteens. The Agent Orange hit the river where we ingested this toxic cocktail.

Thanks Dow and Monsanto, and others who are responsible for the toll of Agent Orange. God will sort out those responsible.

The point of all this is, the effects of all this, coupled with exposure to exotic plants, insects, missions through streams and rivers, the whole jungle experience put stress on the human system. It would take out those with a weak immune system. As they say, only the strong survive. Agent Orange has proven to be a major killer of soldiers from every side. The jungle provided a variety of killers with the usual suspects like Malaria, intense fevers, Black syph with no cure. Black syph wasn't from the jungle, but it was from the enemy girls. Some of these took you out with no warning.

At Yokosuka, a hospital bed seemed strange. It was difficult to adjust to after sleeping on the ground for so long. My Navy doctor approached by skin disease with caution because of my exposure to so many elements. He took many scrapings of my skin, which were put on slides and examined by a microscope. After completion of this process, he then prescribed Grifulvin and Painted Water for external use. Now let me point this out. At the time my Navy doctor prescribed those things, I was still in service, therefore it was service connected. I say this over and over because after I rotated out, the WBH became very real.

The areas on my body were swollen and bleeding like some flesh-eating monster had attacked me. I left Yokosuka Naval Hospital and soon was given an early out, since what was the government going to do with a crazy, sick Marine? In my possession were my prescription bottles while at Yokosuka. The bottles had serial numbers, names, dates, location and everything that proved I was there, and still in service. Soon I ran out of my prescription medications - the same ones Dr Snodgrass prescribed me at Yokosuka. Again, I was still in service, therefore service connected. One more important factor was that I never had to prove the link to Agent Orange. My condition is service connected beyond any doubt. Whether it was Agent Orange, some exotic plant, bad water or a combination of them makes no difference. The main point is I contracted this disease while serving my country in Vietnam.

So I decided to go to my local VA hospital in Indianapolis as an outpatient for inpatient treatment and get my prescriptions refilled - the same ones Dr Snodgrass prescribed while I was in Yokosuka Naval Hospital. All I wanted was my prescription refilled. I wasn't looking for compensation, just basic treatment. Simple right? This is where We've Been Had comes into play. I handed my prescription bottle to the rep at the VA hospital - my hard, physical evidence - clearly marked for them with my name, doctor name and serial number to see. The authenticity of my prescription bottle could easily be verified. The VA rep returned with the most asinine lie, stating there was no record of me ever being treated for this skin disease in Yokosuka Naval Hospital. Initially I laughed in his face. I told this VA vulture, "I just handed you hard, physical evidence with all the recorded data, easily verifiable with a simple phone call to Yokosuka." I told them to get my doctor on the phone, yet The VA rep still denied that I had ever been treated.

I went into full jungle mode and soon I was surrounded by hospital security. I wasn't even given the benefit of the doubt when this VA vulture is holding in his hand enough evidence to win in any court in this land; except against a broken and corrupt VA system. I was physically thrown out of the VA hospital and they recommended I seek help in the private sector. Are you feeling by now the WBH factor? Is it sinking in yet?

This is just what I didn't need, considering when I landed at the airport in California, I saw and heard the protesters cheering at the flag-draped coffins coming down the belt. The atmosphere in America was explosive and the last thing it needed was thousand of warriors, suffering with PSTD and struggling with the effects of war, not even knowing the depths of PTSD.

PTSD was hidden from the soldier and public at large. PTSD surfaced in a mighty way, like a volcano and there's nothing you can do about it. The vulture culture knew there was a serious problem with Vietnam vets, because many were committing high crimes. The prison system was swelling with Vietnam vets, as many were charged with murder, selling and taking drugs among other crimes. Marriages were failing at an alarming rate. The number of homeless was off the charts. Suicides among Vietnam veterans were occurring at an alarming rate. Changing jobs like most would change their underwear. Some went ahead and wiped out their leadership on their way out of a company. These are just a few examples of the impact of the molten lava and its path of destruction.

The VA system has a responsibility to the veteran and the public at large. Many lives could have been saved, but the VA chose a path of denial and turned a blind eye to the volcano right in front of their faces. So the blood of many is to their charge. This VA system chose to become vultures and assassins, changing allegiances to the mighty dollar, rather to the freedom fighters that have made our country so great. Today, that same blind eye and pattern can be easily recognized as PTSD is at epidemic proportions, coupled with suicide rates hitting new highs.

Common sense screams, "What did the VA know and learn from the Vietnam veterans?" Where is the learning curve? Why didn't the VA have programs in place within the private industry like deprogramming, counseling and re-entry programs? The list goes on and on. How could you, the VA, not be ready to deal with suicide PTSD, homeless veterans and veterans having tough times getting jobs? The dollar is king and still rules. The Vulture Assassins are dug in and committed to stop the cost of post war charges.

In my case, I went to the private sector to seek help with my skin disease. I had no choice. I went to private sector skin specialists, who had no idea what was attacking my body. Most of them focused on acne problems and minor psoriasis. Each specialist prescribed the same prescription as my Navy doctor had. The expense was extremely high and there was no relief or solution to my problem. My father, Richard Mitchell decided to step in and help me. He began writing Senators and Congressmen on my behalf. When I came home, this skin problem was all over me and my family knew beyond all doubt that it was linked to the Vietnam War - therefore service connected.

Dad wrote heads of the VA like Richard Roudebush, Senator Vance Hartke, Burch Bayh and so on. Finally, after three years we got a VA hearing. In the hearing was their VA doctor named Dr Navarro. At the time of the hearing, my foot and legs were swollen and bleeding, three years after rotating out of service.

I had already lost two good union jobs. One was with a construction company, but I missed too many days due to the fact that I could not wear my construction boots because of the swelling and bleeding. When I lost that job, I lost my apartment, which put me in the homeless category. Another union job was at Wonder Bread bakery, where I worked the hot bread ovens. This simulated jungle conditions, which flared up my skin condition. We had to wear white uniforms. When schools would come by for tours of the facility, many of the children asked why my white uniform was spotted with blood. In a union shop, each job is by seniority, so it was decided that the sight of blood all over my uniform was not acceptable. Once again, the paychecks ceased, so that meant the inability to pay rent. Wow, homeless again!

The VA doctor, Dr. Navarro was Filipino, so he was very familiar with the tropics and countries like Vietnam. He examined me in the hearing and stated the following:

"Due to the laws that govern Navy physicians, Steve's Navy doctor, Dr. Snodgrass, must first take scrapings of the infected areas and put the slides under a microscope before he could prescribe the drug Grifulvin (which is only for severe cases and is quite potent)."

Dr. Navarro also stated that my Navy doctor MUST input in my records all treatment and prescriptions. "Due to the laws that govern Navy doctors". This is a law! Dr. Navarro also stated that what he saw on my body was similar to what he'd seen in the tropics like Vietnam and the Philippines. Keep in mind that at the time of this hearing, Agent Orange had not been out in the open yet. Also note that I don't have to prove the link to Agent Orange! My case is about service connection! I was treated and given prescriptions BY MY NAVY DOCTOR, Dr. Snodgrass at Yokosuka Naval Hospital while I was still in service.

We wrapped up the VA hearing with a ruling of "Due to a lack of written evidence in Steve's medical records, we are going to deny your claim."

Whatever happened to if there is a reasonable doubt; it should always go in favor of the veteran? This was an illegal ruling. These Vulture Assassins earned their bonuses on this ruling. Why put a veteran through more needless hell when the facts and evidence scream for closure? The link to service connection, overwhelming hard evidence and facts tilted the scale to 100% in my favor. What did the VA have?

This corrupt VA had access to my Navy doctor and could have verified it all with just a simple phone call to Dr. Snodgrass. None of this was done, because the VA is made up of vultures and assassins. My fight did not end there, and my fight continues against this corrupt system. The jungle taught me one thing and that was to continue fighting. Today, after forty two years, yes, forty two years and the fight is still on. I will win this fight because I am right. This broken and corrupt VA system must be dismantled and set right again.

******

All that being said, I will leave this chapter on this note - When you're weary from battle, your inner strength is weak and the fight seems to overwhelm and overtake you - there is hope. Because it isn't over until god says it's over. There is one that came that we may have life and have life more abundantly, and his name is Jesus. There is mucho on the tracks of life and death and you can choose. My true heart and path belong to God and my destiny, purpose and higher plan are in God's hands. You must never forget that as well. The physical and mental damage will not stand.

When you are pounded in life and it seems the bombardment and incoming rounds are relentless, know this - God has his fire mission ready, and when HE fires for effect it is eternal, thorough and a complete victory! The supernatural fire missions carry an anointing to take you into new realms of opportunity, touching those who badly need the fire and desire victory.

Come out of the other side, standing in newness, freedom and a reason to shout Glory to God!

You've become a Soldier of Fortune because you've found the treasure in Christ.

Ephesians 4:22-24:

"You were taught, with regard to your former way of life, to put off your old self, which is being corrupted by its deceitful desires; to be made new in the attitude of your minds; and to put on the new self, created to be like God in true righteousness and holiness."

O.M.D. (OH MY DREAM)

Because of my two year enlistment into the service, I felt as though I had my plan all set up and in place. I'd do my tour, get out and go to college. From there, I'd earn my degree in business and start living my successful life. I knew the burden of paying for college was on my shoulders alone, since Dad's horses hadn't and probably wouldn't come in. Luckily, I was able to secure the GI Bill, which would pay for my college. The dream was in motion.

Unfortunately, the dream took an almost immediate turn once I made it back to the States. After being discharged, I spent some time in Chicago with Junior, catching up and planning my future. I made it back home, got my paperwork in order and enrolled at IUPUI in Indianapolis, with my sights on business. Through the GI Bill, they told me I had three years of college paid for. One thing I knew for certain; I wouldn't be late to class. In Vietnam, many courses had already been served to me. I had a steady diet of discipline, choked down the wake up calls and drank my fill of routine. The wake up calls consisted of superiors busting in, making loud noises, getting physical and calling us everything but our real names. So getting up in time for school would not be an issue.

But a strange thing happened once I started school; I was unable to concentrate. I'd find my body sitting in a lecture hall, but my mind would be back in the jungle. I was totally out of my element. I'd sit for hours in class, but be unable to remember what was discussed. I couldn't retain anything. The military prepared me for study. After all, we'd study maps, terrain, formations and tactics. I was in my element. But when it came to studying and retaining basic mathematics or history, I couldn't pick it up. I'd sit for hours reading and reading and not remember what I had just read. My dream was dying.

We'd never been decontaminated, so to speak from the horrors of war once we returned to civilian life. Over there, it "don't mean nothin'". The worries of civilian life didn't concern us. Once you've come close to stepping on a land mine, or nearly had your head taken off by an AK47, you really don't worry about car payments. Once you've stared death in the face, you don't really think much about your credit report, or when the rent check is due. There was never any integration back into real life, and it was deteriorating my dream. Even today, many dreams are dying in the deserts of Iraq and in the mountains of Afghanistan; and many soldiers don't even know it.

Quickly my grades went downhill. Because I could barely retain anything, I struggled on tests. I'd find myself trying to remember certain math equations, and suddenly thinking about the day at the river. I was almost immediately put on academic probation, and like my first day in the jungle when the Lieutenant said, "Leave the new guy", I got angry. I knew I had to keep my dream alive by any means necessary. But college clearly was not for me. I trudged through it for well over a year, but it was simply for the money I was receiving from the VA. That was my apartment money. My car payment. My survival. I tried to find new ways to sandbag and cut corners to get my degree. Unfortunately, I was in over my head. There was no way around it. But as I said before, I started to get angry.

Another thing taught to us by the war was how to adapt and improvise. In the jungle, we had no choice. When faced with a situation over there, it takes split-second timing to get your bearings straight and make necessary changes to survive. In the situation I found myself in at college, I had to do the same; adapt and improvise. So I adapted, and then I improvised. I left school in the dust and didn't look back.

I worked a few odd jobs in the mean time. I did a little bit of construction work, but due to the Agent Orange poisoning, my feet would swell up and I couldn't wear my work boots. It didn't take long for me to lose that job. I went to work for Wonder Bread and again, the Agent Orange would cause me to bleed through the white uniforms. That was unsanitary, so I lost that job as well. I was getting angrier by the day, and I had to do something to change my situation.

I had no idea what I was going to do next. My mind was still damaged from the war and I had no plan. College had failed. I couldn't hold a job. So I circled the wagons and tried to figure out how I could keep the dream alive. I knew I was good at war. I was good at killing. I was good at planning and adapting. So I got the bright idea in my head that I would become a mercenary. Yeah, that's it! I'll go kill people for money. I heard through the grapevine that some Vietnam vets were doing the same in Africa. But Africa didn't appeal to me. I wasn't really into their war. Who knew what was really going on over there? I didn't, and I didn't care. One country that did appeal to me was Israel. They had the best army, the best soldiers and their country was in turmoil. I could definitely help them. I had skills that they needed. I was a killing machine. They had just gotten past the October War over there, and got pretty chewed up. So what did I do?

I scoured through the phone book and started calling synagogues, offering my services. That should tell you immediately how insane I was at the time. I mean, who does that?

"Hey my name's Steve Mitchell and I'm a Vietnam vet. Yeah, I see you guys are in a lot of trouble and I hear you guys could use some mercenaries over there. I'm real good at war and I could stack some bodies for you if you'd like. So uh, how do I get over there?"

::click::

Click after click, actually. A couple of them told me that I could go over there and be a part of a kibitz, and then from there I'd be able to secure contacts to get in business. I didn't want to do that. I wanted to get right to the killing. They had to have thought I was out of my mind, or even trying to set them up. I was actually calling people and asking if I could go kill people for them. Needless to say, that idea fell apart from the jump. To this day, I sometimes still think about that and shake my head that I had tried something so insane.

Then one Sunday, I was scouring the want ads in the local paper. Several ads caught my eye. One specifically was the word "logistics". I was good at logistics. After all, logistics is pretty much planning, adapting and improvising. Logistics was for me, there was no doubt about it. So I began looking at ads seeking logistics professionals, and many seeking logistical professionals were also seeking buyers. Many of the ads had the same specific needs. Planning, logistics, supply chain - these were all the things I learned in the jungle. If a base camp needed more supplies, it got ordered. It seemed pretty simple to me. I could do this. This was not going to be an issue; keep the supply line filled and if something needed to be bought, I'd buy it.

So I sat down and began to piece together a resume', taken from the various ads I found seeking buyers. I researched companies who had gone out of business, so my background story could not be verified. I created a pretty good resume' out of thin air and started sending them out. I was now a buyer, with an extensive background in logistics and vast experience in supply chain.

It wasn't long before I was called into an interview with American Can Corporation. Of course, they were blown away by my fake resume'. I did my best to retain as much information as I could on what a buyer did, so I aced the interview. I charmed the pants off of them by adapting and improvising. They loved me. So they offered me a job as a buyer, making very good money.

I didn't really think things through though. Now that I had the job, I had responsibilities as a buyer. Unfortunately, I didn't have the experience. I was in over my head, and needed to figure a way to adapt, improvise and sandbag. I easily made friends at ACC, and that included a guy who had obviously been in the business a while. When faced with a tough situation, I'd pick his brain. I'd let him know that from my past "experience", we'd do things a certain way and ask his advice on how he would do it. He was always very forthcoming with information, and from there, I'd pick up procedures and figure out how to do my job. I'd also find others in the company who were seeking to climb the ladder, and pass my work off onto them under the guise that I was just too swamped to handle such petty requests for reports. Everyone was very willing to do my work for me. I had them duped. I was

sandbagging and was good at it. After a short amount of time, I was able to pick up on my own what I needed to be a successful buyer; and I was a very good buyer.

I had a nice apartment on the North side of Indianapolis. I had the best furniture and a killer stereo system. I was well on my way to fulfilling my dream. The American Dream was finally mine. That was shortly before the "Hood" was pulled over my head in the form of an old friend named Bob Hood, who would soon take me on an adventure that I'd never forget.

BOB HOOD AND "LA EME"

I was finally living the dream on the North side of Indy. I had secured myself a great job as a buyer with American Can Corporation and had a luxury apartment with plenty of spending money. Life was good. Life was actually really good. But that all changed when I got a knock on my door one evening. I answered the door to find my old buddy, Bob Hood standing there with his Mexican girlfriend.

Bob Hood was a bad dude. He ran around the neighborhood where I grew up. He was a red haired guy, about 6 foot tall and 175 pounds of muscle. From the look of him, you'd never imagine that he'd be able to rip your head off at the shoulders. But he could. Bob was a door gunner in the Army during Vietnam, earning a Bronze Star. He was legit.

I met Bob around 1964 when I was in high school at Arsenal Tech. Bob went to

Howe high school, and was a member of a street gang called the "Howe Barons". The Howe Barons were a pretty tough street gang, and one that didn't hesitate to bash your face in if they saw fit. I was a fighter, too. But even I knew not to mess with any of the Howe Barons.

Unfortunately, my friend Rick Thompson did. I don't recall how it started, but there was supposed to be a scheduled fight between Rick and Bob a few days from then. Knowing how the Barons operated, I knew it wasn't going to be one on one. Rick was a dead man, and I made sure he knew it. Of course, Rick was in a panic. He didn't know what to do and asked for my help. I didn't know what to do either. It wasn't like I was friends with any of them. But I told him I would see what I could do. So I put a word out on the street that I wanted a meeting with Bob. Well, word got back to Bob, and we met to talk. I explained that Rick was no match for him and the Barons, and for some reason he took a real liking to me, even asking me if I wanted to join the gang. I declined, but we settled everything then and there, I asked him to call off the fight and Rick was off the hook. From there, Bob and I remained friends.

Back in Indiana after the war, word got to Bob that I was back in town. He was just back from the war as well, and decided to look me up. So he shows up at my door one night with a beautiful Mexican girl in tow and we catch up.

Bob tells me he's working now for a guy named Bobby out of Brownsville, Texas, and tells me he's forming a team. A team? What kind of team? A drug running team, that is. He had a third guy already in place who would handle the Chicago/Detroit market. Bob and I would handle the state of Indiana. The plan was to take loads of marijuana from Brownsville to Indianapolis, and from Indy, we'd set up our network. Bob already had an apartment set up for us in Corpus Christi, and we'd base out of there. I also found out that Bobby was a member of "La Eme", or as many refer to it as the Mexican Mafia. Bob was the liaison to Bobby and I liked it that way. I didn't want to meet Bobby or know anything about him, and I never did meet him. Bob tells me he can start me at 2 grand a week and hands me a .45 pistol with the serial numbers rubbed off. It was good to feel the grip of a .45 in my hands again. I was in. I was in with both feet. My only question was when do we start?

Pretty quickly, actually. I left my apartment and everything in it and we set up our operation with precision. Bobby had a large factory down there in Brownsville, where they'd brick up the pot nicely. It was always wrapped tight in brown paper and tied together, and we'd move hundreds of pounds of it at a time. It was always the best pot around. When we'd open the bags, it would just expand out with gold buds everywhere. So we had no problem selling our top grade weed to anyone who wanted it. I looked at this as just another mission, just like I did in Vietnam. Planning, adapting and improvising were always used to keep the mission running. We kept our loads tight and always knew what was out there and where.

In Indianapolis, we rented high end executive homes and set them up as our stash houses. We were getting some of the best pot a pothead could hope for. Kush,

Kind bud, you name it. Every once in a while Bob could get us a load of Acapulco Gold. But our weed was the best. I began to network with friends in the Indianapolis area to move lots of pot. I had a contact at Indiana State University, and he was able to move many pounds for me and direct me to a guy at Indiana University who could move pounds as well. My brother Jimmy had his network of friends. I also got in touch with Jay and Tom, who were old friends, and let me tell you, their friends could smoke a lot of weed. So the connections were really growing at a rapid rate. I wasn't a nickel and dimer. I wanted to move pounds at a time, since it was less work for me. The demand at Indiana State was huge. I'd drop off 5 to 10 pounds of it at a time, sometimes more. I also hooked up with a big fraternity there. They would sell it to their friends and so on. Our little cartel was starting to grow. Too fast actually, as when you have a lot out there, it gets hard to keep track of it sometimes. Bob was starting to get reckless too. With missions like this, you have to keep a low profile. With so much of our stuff out there, if someone gets busted, the cops are going to ask where they got it from, and so on. If you are brazen and flashy, it's only a matter of time before the cops showed up on your doorstep.

So Bob was the typical flashy drug dealer. So much that he would even tell people he was one. He wore the white shirt unbuttoned to the navel, with gold chains and wads of cash. I remember once we ended up at a car dealership on the East side and he bought a brand new Riviera with cash. I went ballistic. I angrily asked him if he was trying to get us busted. Bob, you can't do that! Are you out of your mind? He'd always tell me to calm down and not to worry, but he was just one that couldn't be reasoned with. He made me nervous with his flashy lifestyle. A few months after we started, we were in Brownsville getting ready to bring a load to Indy and we got word that the third member of the team was killed in a motorcycle accident in Indianapolis. I didn't know the guy, but he and Bob were close. Bob fell apart. He smoked pot the whole way back to Indy, crying about his dead friend. Like before, I went nuts. I mean, we're moving hundreds of pounds of pot and if we're busted, it's a life sentence. He's got the windows down and smoking it! Reckless, I tell ya. That's why I kept the .45 nearby and always made sure the brake lights and everything else on the car or truck were working. I didn't need to get pulled over by the cops. I was also fully prepared to be in a shoot out with whoever tried to hijack us. So Bob's putting us in a real bad place by blazing the whole way home. Luckily, we made it back without being stopped.

You always have people trying to cheat you and rip you off, too. I knew my brothers wouldn't try to rip me off. But that's not to say their friends wouldn't try to rip them off, which did happen sometimes. I remember Jimmy got ripped off a couple times, but what could I do? He was my brother. It's not like I could pop a cap in him. I ran into a little problem once and almost had to make a crazy decision. Tom and Jay were always moving for me. I knew I could trust them since they were old friends. There was also a guy that we grew up with named Dubby. Dubby was a goofy fat guy who always read comic books, but man could he smoke grass. He wanted in on a piece of the action. I didn't really like Dubby, but I trusted Tom and Jay, so I reluctantly agreed. Suddenly, Dubby was getting ripped off a lot. I had to put a stop to it.

I ended up at Tom and Jay's not long after, and Dubby showed up. I asked him where my money was. He hemmed and hawed about getting ripped off and whatnot. Well, I'd had enough. So I pulled out my .45 and put it to his head. I told him I wanted my money or I was gonna kill him, and I would have too. Tom and Jay freaked out and Dubby was a mess. But somehow, he was able to miraculously come up with my money. Dubby was out at that point, needless to say.

When you have a network and are moving so much pot, you run into quite a few problems. One of which is, what do you do with the money? In the beginning, we'd just tape the money to Bob and fly him down to Brownsville where he'd drop the money off. Soon we couldn't do that since we were moving so many loads. The second of which is, as I mentioned before, being ripped off or hijacked. Hijackings happened often on the road. The word gets out in the underworld that people are moving massive loads of pot, which we were definitely doing. So much that we had to buy boats and trailers to move the tons of pot up the pipeline. It gets hairy when both problems hit you at once.

Every month or so after we started getting really big, two Mexican enforcers would come to Indianapolis and we'd meet at the Holiday Inn bar to drop off the money. I didn't like these guys at all. They were scary. Quiet scary. These were not guys to be messing with. They'd come up, we'd meet and Bob would handle all the talking. I didn't talk to them at all. Let's just dispense with the pleasantries, give them the money, plan the next load and keep rolling. That was my idea. Yeah, not Bob.

Bob got a bright idea to start skimming money from Bobby. What an insane idea. You don't steal from the Mexican Mafia. He'd tell Bobby's men that he got hijacked on the way to Indy and he'd keep the money. I told him it was stupid to do that, as we were making good money and we didn't need to be greedy. Not to mention, these enforcers would kill us, our families and our dogs and not bat an eyelash. It didn't faze Bob. So I was getting nervous. He was flashy, he talked a lot and things are starting to unravel. So Bob skims a load. He made up a story about being hijacked, and Bobby let it slide. The second time, he wasn't as understanding.

At this point, I have one foot out the door. Bob and I had a huge argument that almost escalated to a fist fight. Bob was just too loud, too flashy. The DEA was onto us, as when we'd meet at the Holiday Inn bar, there they'd be just a few tables away. Did that quiet Bob down? Of course not. He kept talking. So Bob and I are arguing and I told him my phone was tapped and I wanted out. The DEA was onto us and it was a matter of time before they took us down. I told him I was done and we parted ways. That was it. I walked away. I took my money, found another place to live and went on with my life. I didn't see Bob for another several years after that. Unfortunately for Bob, things would get worse for him, as he tried to skim Bobby one time too many.

I didn't hear about the incident until many years later, sitting inside Dove Recording Studio in Indianapolis with my friend, Skip. Who would come strolling through but my old friend, Bob? But he wasn't strolling very well. He was walking with a cane due to a limp and had a fake ear. As we started to talk, I could tell that something wasn't right with him.

Apparently a short time after he and I parted ways, he decided to skim a load from Bobby again. I guess Bobby wasn't willing to look the other way this time. He sent his two enforcers to Indianapolis for a face to face talk with Bob. But there was little talking. They first shot Bob in the knee with a high powered rifle. Clearly, Bobby had wanted him to suffer a bit before they killed him. They then shot him in the right side of the head, which blew off part of the top of his head. Thinking he was dead, they cut his ear off to take back to Bobby as proof they killed him. I was floored. I couldn't believe that all happened! Not long after that, Bob turned State's evidence on Bobby and his crew, and they went on to do hard time in prison.

Imagine my surprise when Bob looked to me and said, "That contract was for you too, brother!"

Once again, "The Edge" was there for me, and I didn't even know it.

PTSD

Post-traumatic stress disorder (PTSD) is a severe anxiety disorder that can develop after exposure to any event that results in psychological trauma. This event may involve the threat of death to oneself or to someone else, or to one's own or someone else's physical, sexual, or psychological integrity, overwhelming the individual's ability to cope. As an effect of psychological trauma, PTSD is less frequent and more enduring than the more commonly seen acute stress response. Diagnostic symptoms for PTSD include re-experiencing the original trauma(s) through flashbacks or nightmares, avoidance of stimuli associated with the trauma, and increased arousal – such as difficulty falling or staying asleep, anger, and hyper-vigilance. Formal diagnostic criteria require that the symptoms last more than one month and cause significant impairment in social, occupational, or other important areas of functioning. Post-traumatic stress disorder is classified as an anxiety disorder, characterized by aversive anxiety-related experiences, behaviors, and physiological responses that develop after exposure to a psychologically traumatic event (sometimes months after). Its features persist for longer than 30 days, which distinguishes it from the briefer acute stress disorder. These persisting posttraumatic stress symptoms cause significant disruptions of one or more important areas of life function. It has three sub-forms: acute, chronic, and delayed-onset.

It was twenty years too late in the late 80s when I was called into the VA hospital for a PTSD test. Now, this was the same VA hospital that I was thrown out of by security, and what was my crime? I thought I could get basic treatment and my prescriptions refilled. The same prescriptions my Navy doctor, Dr. Snodgrass prescribed for a flesh eating, severe skin disease I contracted in the jungles of Vietnam and Cambodia. I shouldn't mention Cambodia, because the game was that we were never there. Wow.

The lies governments tell make you wonder how they can sort out the Pat Tillman tragedy or the Osama Bin Laden mission. It took our government twenty years to figure out the Vietnam vets were blowing a gasket, and once again there was no blowout preventers, as the Vietnam war got away from everyone. We punished everyone when we got home. Innocent bystanders, family authority figures, copes, bosses, girlfriends and wives; no one was safe, including us. Never has our country been to war where one generation of veterans turned on another. The American public, politicians and everyone else was blaming the wrong group. The Vietnam vets were sent by our country. Some patriots went to

Canada or Russian or even hid out in college as the war escalated and unraveled. Some of us Marines and many others cut out our own war and laid down our own rules of engagement. We tailored some of our strategies on our own, and not tied to any book.

For some reason, Vietnam vets were still pulling the trigger. An alarm bell sounded as so-called citizens wanted the problems to go away. The suicide rate was spiraling out of control. But we were doing our best to stop the pain. Prisons were swelling with Vietnam vets who were infected with PTSD. But the government tried to downplay PTSD, due to the fact that it was linked to the Treasury Department. Bodies were strewn from coast to coast and our government had no chance to distance itself from the political fallout that was manifesting all over our nation. The rhetoric was nauseating and dizzying, as voices one after another tried to address what happened to Johnny Soldier as he rotated home from his so-called tour in Vietnam.

Unless you went to Vietnam, there is absolutely no way for you to understand, nor do you have the right to judge the insanity and results of decisions made over there.

The PTSD test was a joke, and I'm sure it temporarily satisfied the cry for results to problems that will take generations to heal. I did not trust the government, as so many of us don't. How many reasons do you want? The quick test was over though. The method of their madness was to run a computer program of all vets who engaged in high combat. I was one of those test batches, and shortly thereafter was awarded 100% disability. At the time, the generosity left me warm and speechless.

My next encounter at the same VA hospital included the full treatment, as I was placed in the PTSD ward. This was in 1994, and we were at the twenty-five year mark. I was told once that the wheels of the government turn slowly. That's clearly an understatement. I was assigned my own psychologist for group sessions, and was assigned a psychiatrist for drugs and oversight. He answered to the head shrink who ran the PTSD program. The tactics they used were to immediately give me drugs three times a day. The lines for medication gave me little hope, as I was slowly drugged enough to take away as much rage and anger as possible. That included taking away the few friends I had.

I had no way of knowing where the mission was heading and I couldn't figure out how those drugs could solve PTSD. I sized up the ward and noticed that most of the people inside looked and acted crazy. The place was loaded with bi-polar schizophrenics, those who suffered from anxiety and panic attacks, sociopaths. Some had even committed serious crimes, and yes, PTSD rounded out the field of rejects. I knew I wasn't like them. I wasn't crazy and I didn't belong there.

They soon got us into our sessions with our psychologists. The woman assigned to me wanted off my case immediately, as she couldn't handle any of what I was giving her. I was given to the "Dirty Harry" of psychologists, Dr. Pfenniger. This guy was seasoned and he could handle complex cases. I did like him because he was tough. After several weeks I was getting restless. If there was any progress, I could not see it. My handlers all had different views on what my future would be. The head psychiatrist wanted to send me out of state and wanted them to throw away the key. My wife had only to sign the papers. Then, behind this door I was scheduled for a round table parlay that included staff members, psychologists and all the way up the chain. This meeting was to determine my fate.

I was on a pay phone early on and a rude patient wanted to use the phone. He screamed at me at the top of his lungs repeatedly. Finally I snapped. I dropped the phone and hit him in the neck with the side of my hand. He hit the floor. Several nurses who liked me got me out of there in a hurry. Security came, strapped the man down and put him on lock down. Now, I have a dilemma when that guy is released. It was over for me, but I wasn't the one strapped down to a gurney.

The conclusion from the medical crop of geniuses was that they had to kick me out of the ward because I was too violent. I replied that I thought that was the reason why I was there in the first place. Well, they discharged me anyway. I'm sorry to say that recently after I was released, the head psychiatrist there committed suicide, as he was going to lose his job due to downsizing.

Dr. Pfenniger, who gave it his best shot and upon my release, sat on his therapy couch crying and left my wife with a departing statement – "Mrs. Mitchell, there's nothing more we can do for Steve." According to them, I could not be helped any further. I figured he was probably right, and I'd just have to do the best that I could as I always had. The Edge would provide a program that continues even today – It's not over until God says it's over. The one who heals your body and mind had no problem with the maniac of the Gadarenes in Luke 8:26. So he'd surely not have a problem with me. I am no expert, but "I Am" gives me the edge to carry fire and anointing to touch those in need.

*****

One learns quickly that the war does not wind down, but heats up in the vast jungle of your soul. It waits to inflict a new toll and keep you a prisoner to the past. Freedom can be found in three words – God Help Me! Liberation is up to you. It is your call. Each war has its own traumas and realities. Just when you think you've made it out of hell, it pulls you back in where the torment starts with Survivor's guilt. Coming out of the chaos of war summons many voices of contradiction and confusion. You've made it out, but why are you so disappointed? There is a voice that says, "I must get out of here" and a voice that says, "I must go back." There is an intense battle within the soul as the individual tries to work it out internally with no success. The hunger and desire for a new chapter in one's life eats away at an individual. With each step, traps are set within the mind to pull you back, releasing flashbacks of pain and misery. They literally keep you on the same path. As you attempt to gather strength to regroup, the enemy attacks in the night with rapid-fire precision. The nightmares hit the mark and remind you of the horrors of war. This continues and keeps you chained in the war zone.

Like a brain freeze grips you in the head, so do the traumatic events that lock you up in a split second. Just like freeze pops that cause that non lethal condition, PTSD takes us to our limits. PTSD is a dream killer and a destiny changer.

I came back home to the land of the free and the home of the brave. But nothing felt free and it sure didn't feel like home. Restlessness is also a part of the post package. You desire a break from the action, yet miss it at the same time. The battles rage within the mind as you replay each occurrence, hoping for a new outcome. Satan's battlefield shoots for permanent damage and hopefully, death. The night sweats and the sounds and smells of war fill your body, mind, ears and nostrils anew every night. A sound mind seems out of reach. There's a continual struggle for your identity, because no one knows you anymore. A new day beings the same; reruns of old days, and the beat goes on.

Take into account pro surfer Steph Gilmore, who at 22 years old was invincible. She was known in the surfing world as "Happy Gilmore" because of her joyous demeanor. She had just been crowned ASP world champion for the fourth year in a row, and was fresh off a Triple Crown title. Weeks away from announcing a move to Quiksliver, where she would become teammates with 10 time world champion Kelly Slater, and sign a 5 million dollar contract, her life would change in an instant as she was going through life's motions. She was heading home to her apartment, and as she arrived, she noticed a shoeless man wandering around her carport. No reason to be afraid, she told herself. Suddenly her eyes meet his for an instant. Next comes the feeling that something isn't right. A few more steps and he was sprinting towards her with a metal bar in his hand. Before she could react, he was on top of her. She suffered a deep gash on her head, broke her wrist and tore ligaments in her hand. He was caught later that night and his motives were unclear.

After that, Gilmore didn't want to go home anymore. She did return home eventually, but only left for trips to the doctor and to the police station. Friends took turns staying with her and calmed her when she woke with nightmares. She didn't sleep alone for months. Only recently has she felt comfortable enough to be alone. Her first focus was the physical recovery. She thought she could separate life and sports, just like a soldier thinks he can separate life and war. Reality set in as she paddled out for her first heat, just like it set in for me my first day in college. She couldn't find her rhythm. She couldn't tap into her confidence. That's what PTSD does to you. It saps your energy and leaves you feeling that there is no way out.

Elite athletes see themselves as special and invincible. Elite soldiers see themselves in much the same way. Steph faced danger all the time, but she adapted and overcame. The war veteran does the same. Monica Seles still struggles with PTSD after a crazed Steffi Graf fan stabbed her in the back during a break in a match. A split second of horror fundamentally changed her as a person, just as it did Steph, me and countless other war veterans. After the attack, she quit playing tennis.

This is the ripple effect from the horrors of war or brutal trauma. You drop out, you dig deep and you avoid people and stressors. The greatest challenge is to regain the perspective you had before the trauma. For many of us, it's just not possible. It is much more than a lost perspective. Trying to find that spot again can sometimes take a lifetime.

What is the answer?

The Edge.

In war, there is little mercy. With Satan, there is none. The cycle of chaos has an agenda, and that is to take you out. Suicide is the vehicle. I tell you this because I've been there. I've been to the very edge. But praise God, I now have "The Edge". I have the rock. It all started with those three words;

"God, Help Me!"

Our answer to victorious living starts with staying stirred up and mindful, and we do that by keeping our minds full of the word of God.

Romans 12:1-2 says

Therefore, I urge you, brothers and sisters, in view of God's mercy, to offer your bodies as a living sacrifice, holy and pleasing to God – this is your true and proper worship. Do not conform to the pattern of this world, but be transformed by the renewing of your mind. Then you will be able to test and approve what God's will is – his good, pleasing and perfect will.

We must first submit ourselves to the Lord. By saying those three words, "God, Help me!" we draw ourselves near to him in submission. We acknowledge to him that we cannot do it on our own. We let him know we need his help. So many athletes and soldiers believe they can do it on their own. They cannot. Monica Seles, Steph Gilmore and me are three examples of that. Once we submit and seek his help, he then can begin and thereafter continue to complete his work in us. We must be transformed in our minds, and we do that by seeking him through his word. There are many words of encouragement and healing, and they are all ours for the taking.

Hebrews 10:16-17

This is the covenant that I will make with them after those days, says the Lord, I will put my laws into their hearts, and in their minds will I write them; And their sins and iniquities will I remember no more.

We will be fully enlightened and have the perfect knowledge of the truth. All our affections, passions and appetites will be purified so we can willingly obey his word. He will no longer remember the sins of the past. He will make us new creations.

2 Corinthians 5:17

Therefore if any man be in Christ, he is a new creature: old things are passed away; behold all things have become new.

All things become new. Our minds become new. Our thinking becomes new. The soulish nature – the mind, the will and the emotions are now new. The wounds of the hearts and minds are now old. They're in the past. Forgotten. The peace of God which passes all understanding will guard our hearts and minds through Christ Jesus (Philippians 4:17). All we need to do is cry out those three words.

"GOD, HELP ME!"

We will find rest in our souls (Matthew 11:29) and no longer be blinded by Satan (2 Cornthians 4:4). We can be re-wired from the traumas of war, with a new mind that can only be relieved by God and his word. We can have a new mind, a new will and new emotions.

So what is our action? We must look, listen and believe. We must pray! The enemy will certainly attempt to clutter our minds with distractions and throw misdirection plays our way. But we must stay guarded and equipped to stand against the enemy and his tricks. Pray for your mind. Use that same fighting spirit and attitude used in war time to war against the enemy. God is the God of more. So we should not settle for less.

Jeremiah 32:27

"Behold, I am the Lord, the God of all flesh. Is there anything too hard for me?"

Is PTSD too hard for him? Is Agent Orange? What about Gulf War Syndrome?

Plain and simple? No. Don't let the battle you're in change your mind from the truth. Vietnam vets – whatever state you're in with your mind and body - Chains need to and can be broken. God can do it! His word is like fire. It is like a hammer that breaks rocks into pieces (Jeremiah 23:29). The battle of the mind needs a hammer. That hammer is the almighty Word of God. Many

Vietnam vets were declared outcasts. But the truth is, we were sent.

Jeremiah 30:17

For I will restore health unto thee, and I will heal thee of thy wounds, says the LORD; because they called thee an outcast, saying, This is Zion, whom no man seeks after.

We also need to keep our minds on the tasks at hand. When we set up in the jungle, we set our perimeter, dug in and prepared ourselves for the onslaught that awaited us. The same goes in our spiritual battles. God places spiritual warfare partners around us to help guard our 360. Our focus should be our own spiritual kill zone, if you will. In the jungle, we couldn't get caught up in the kill zones of our fellow soldiers. Such is the same in our spiritual perimeter. Trust the skills and battle readiness of those placed in our spiritual 360. For if we begin to look around us at what our fellow spiritual warriors are battling, we lose sight on our own focus, and we begin to spray the 360 around us. In the jungle, that results in friendly kills. In the spiritual realm, that involves breaking down those who are standing with us, and doing so by our own hands. In other words, when the enemy comes in like a flood, raise up a standard against it - the blood of Jesus - rather than take out our frustrations and aggressions on those who are standing with us in battle! Trust your prayer warriors! If they are overrun with sappers, trust that they have the skills to defeat them. For if you attempt to fire in their kill zone, you could take out one of your own.

Ephesians 6:10-20

Finally, be strong in the Lord and in his mighty power. Put on the full armor of God, so that you can take your stand against the devil's schemes. For our struggle is not against flesh and blood, but against the rulers, against the authorities, against the powers of this dark world and against the spiritual forces of evil in the heavenly realms. Therefore put on the full armor of God, so that when the day of evil comes, you may be able to stand your ground, and after you have done everything, to stand. Stand firm then, with the belt of truth buckled around your waist, with the breastplate of righteousness in place, and with your feet fitted with the readiness that comes from the gospel of peace. In addition to all this, take up the shield of faith, with which you can extinguish all the flaming arrows of the evil one. Take the helmet of salvation and the sword of the Spirit, which is the word of God.

And pray in the Spirit on all occasions with all kinds of prayers and requests. With this in mind, be alert and always keep on praying for all the Lord's people. Pray also for me, that whenever I speak, words may be given me so that I will fearlessly make known the mystery of the gospel, for which I am an ambassador in chains. Pray that I may declare it fearlessly, as I should.

Be strong and courageous. Put on the full armor (My wife, Jackie will show you how to do that in the chapter "Wife of

War") of God. Stand firm, and remember you are not fighting with flesh and blood. As I mentioned before, you are not a Soldier of Fortune anymore. You are a soldier of the most high. Now it's time to stand and act like one!

A WIFE OF WAR, SUIT UP

When a famous author wrote that "Women were from Venus and that Men were from Mars", I don't think he was including the tragedies of war and the effects that most men suffer in some way or another. How to hold your life together after your beloved returns from the unspeakable events of war is not taught to us. My Mother never covered the section on special circumstances so when I was faced with the many changes, to say that I was unequipped to handle it would have been an understatement. However, I have found that the many elements of a women's weaponry can aid in the healing of her husband's soul. I want every wife, mother, sister, niece and girlfriend to know that there is hope and help for recovery. I will tell you of my own experiences, and knowing that God's word says he is not a respecter of persons. Acts 10:34-38, which states, "What he does for one he has made available to all" is a guarantee of his help for you. I grew up watching my friends and family go to Vietnam and then I watched them return, never the same emotionally, some lost limbs, or had scars from shrapnel wounds and many suffered from the effects of being sprayed or exposed to Agent Orange. But one thing was the same for all, they all suffered from P.T.S.D. My family lost a member and I watched as his wife and immediate family changed permanently from the trauma of this tragic loss. Since I was touched by the war, I had great compassion for the warriors; a compassion that would be put to the test of commitment.

When I met my husband Steve I was trying to recover from a divorce. I had my own issues of insecurity, fear and doubt. But we spent hours just talking and getting to know each other. He told me about some of the lighter stories of his war experiences and I told him mine. We connected through this common bond of loss and emotional pain and fell in love. You know when you go through the blind stages of love and you just don't see the signs that might be a problem later? Well I was blind for sure and in retrospect I see where I ignored all the obvious signals he was giving out. I did not know he had P.T.S.D. but that is not something that they can repress or hide. For example, we never went out to the show unless it was the latest one and we never went to dinner until after all the crowds were gone. If he went shopping it was right when the store opened and you had to get in and get right out, no browsing around. He hated loud noise of any kind and could never stand to be startled in any way. I know this might seem little, but try it all the time and see what you think because it gets old. After we were married I began to see the anger in him that would erupt over the smallest things. I had never seen such anger and rage, so I handled it the only way I could think of. I pacified him. I had to always be upbeat. I could not get angry in front of him or show any emotions of sorrow or sadness, and worst of all I had to hide any problems from him, especially finances. Since he was not working more than he was, we were always in debt and in need. The pressure would cause him to be depressed and brood.

He slept so restlessly, when he slept at all. I didn't want to live this way it was such an impossible situation to endure for us both. I had been in painful emotional situations before and there is only one answer. There is only one way to bring peace and joy to your life and that is through Jesus Christ. But since this trauma he suffers did not happen overnight but in layers over time, I knew the healing was not going to be instantaneous. In Romans 12:2 and Ephesians 4:23, it tells us we are to renew our minds. Well, if we have to renew them then they must have been damaged. To renew according to Webster's Dictionary, means to restore, overhaul, reshape or revise. Have you ever stretched anything out of shape? It's not easy to get it to take its proper shape again. You have to work at it, sometimes slowly. Whenever we have trauma you can depend on the enemy being right there in your mind, replaying every single horrifying moment to keep you off balance. Steve was born again and spirit filled but not renewed in his thinking about many things. He had trouble letting go of situations and letting God have the burden. He tried to fix so many things himself without God and this only leads to failure. I was a fixer too, much to the holding back of progress for God. I prayed and I sought God's help for my husband, but I also enabled him by making things seem okay when they were far from it. I did not want to risk his wrath, I wanted to keep him happy and content but all I was doing was stopping the workings of God in our lives. My intentions were good. However, I wasn't putting my trust in God either. This lead to more discord and strife in our home that lead to more covering up the truth and pretending all was well. It all became a cycle of putting a band aid on a bullet hole as they say. But we serve a mighty God, with mighty plans and good intentions for us, if we would only listen. Let's start here, in Ephesians 6:10, it says, *"Finally, my brethren, be strong I the Lord, and in the power of his might."* To me the word "finally" reveals that before this you must have tried other methods, and "be strong in the Lord" is not relying on your own strength because the next words say "in the power of *HIS* might". Again this expresses that it will be God's strength and power that we give us a victory, not our own. Now how do we get to that point where we allow God to do the directing? The answer is *trials and tribulations.* We just love them don't we? We seem to enjoy going around the proverbial barn as many times as possible. Eventually we get it and we learn but not without a fight from our flesh. No matter how many times I would present God with a perfectly good idea or plan, he would never take my advice. Of course that didn't seem to stop me from trying to give it to him. Most of our plans must seem like an idea straight from the Three Stooges to God, but he lovingly and patiently guides us to his will, where we can be safe and protected. Speaking only for myself, I know I must have given God a lot of laughs.

I began to see the healing power of God move for my husband when he had a serious bout of malaria. It seems once you have malaria, you will always have it. It reoccurs and causes the symptoms of fever, and hallucinations. I knew he had it while in Vietnam and another bout of it when he came home, but I had never seen it firsthand. It was an already hot summer day and he had been feeling ill, like the flu, so he went back to bed about mid-morning. I left him alone so that he could sleep after giving him something for a fever. I went about my day with the children and tried to keep the house quiet so that he could sleep. As I checked on him through the day he was getting worse, he fever was increasing, his demeanor was fretful, he refused food or drink and began to shout things at me that made no sense at all. I believe at one point he didn't even know who I was. He began to cry about the dogs needing to be fed and how he had to dig a hole. Well I had no idea what to do for him so I laid my hands on him and began praying. Just as I got him to calm down the Lord spoke to me and told me to cast out the spirit of malaria. Of course I had to hear it about five times before I actually did it because I thought I was going crazy myself. I obeyed the Lord and took authority over the enemy and cast out that demon. Well much to my surprise, my husband got very still, he opened his eyes and smiled at me and asked me what happened. He was totally healed and has never had the slightest reoccurrence of malaria again. Glory be to God! Now God was revealing his mighty hand again, to guide my husband to a road of healing not just his body but his mind. I don't think that Steve knew or understood the love that God had for him. He couldn't love or forgive himself and this would take years to become a reality for him. Steve always wanted to do right, and he was always genuinely sorry for his wrong words and actions. But he never thought he was worth anything to God because of the sins he had committed and because he had been rejected so deeply. His experiences happened one at a time and now God was positioning him to heal him one event at a time.

Even after a decade after being in Vietnam his memories were so fuzzy. Many things he had buried deep inside himself and he never let anyone get to close to help him. His brother once offered to take him to counseling but he flatly refused. He just didn't want to remember. However when God brings back violent and traumatizing memories, it is not to torment us as Satan would but to heal us and "renew" our hearts, minds and emotions. Well God began doing just that. A dear friend and Pastor told my husband that God was going to bring back, not flashback, his forgotten memories in order to heal him. When this process began it was very painful for him, but it was also clarifying and so very refreshing when it was healed. Reliving those events broke him in so many ways. It broke the hate he had for the people he was fighting against and a new compassion rose up within him. He was beginning to see from a "renewed" mind. This process has never ended. God has never stopped helping and healing him. My husband has not always submitted to God's help. He's kind of like that little kid who goes into time out but he is standing up on the inside. Then, when he does allow the hand of God to move, he is always the better for it and like all of us, he wonders why he resisted in the first place. The hardest part was when he had to relive the losses he suffered in the war and after. The comrades he lost and the relationships that crumbled as a result of P.T.S.D. He was the reason so many relationships failed, and the losses caused him to retreat inside himself and harden his heart while he withdrew from anyone who loved him. The men that suffer from P.T.S.D. go through emotional cycles, and it traps them away from what they really want to feel. In relationships they blame, belittle and reject the very individual they love. So you have this cycle of anger and rage and then that turns to sorrow for their actions and trying to repair the damage they caused. All the while growing inside them is a self-hatred for what they cannot stop themselves from doing. But they can stop with the help of our gracious Lord and Savior Jesus Christ, and the will to "renew "their minds.

Though this book covers not only the horrors of war and its aftermath for the soldier, there is a solution which we want to convey to the reader. This chapter is for the fallout victims of P.T.S.D. The mothers, wives, girlfriends and children of soldiers who suffer from the loss of the one who came home changed. How do we survive? How do they learn to cope with the ticking time bomb of anger and rage which now embodies the head of the household? If gone untreated and ignored the results are dysfunction and divorce, and in most cases the children and wives end up with a case of secondary P.T.S.D. and the pain is born again and again in our children and loved ones. This cycle must end. We must spiritually fight with our spiritually weapons and overrun the confusion with direction, wipeout the hate with love and replace the rage with the peace that passes all understanding. This mission calls for the supernatural, yoke destroying, burden removing, power of GOD! It starts with "prayer". It is so great when we pray because we already have Gods word to reassure us that he is there to heal and restore. Psalms 147:3 says "*He heals the brokenhearted and binds up their wounds*". He doesn't think about helping, he helps. You see, as you embark on this quest of recovery you must protect yourself as well, that is why God has provided us with a suit of armor and all of the tools of protection for success.

Remember where we started in Ephesians 6:10? Well, let's finish the instructions of this passage and begin to move in the direction of victory and away from despair.

Ephesians 6:10-18, Finally, my brethren, be strong in the Lord, and in the power of his might. Put on the whole armor of God that you may be able to stand against the wiles (methods) of the devil. For we wrestle not against flesh and blood, but against principalities and powers, against the rulers of the darkness of this age, against spiritual hosts of wickedness in the heavenly places. Therefore take up the WHOLE armor of God that you may be able to stand in the evil day, and having done all to stand. Stand therefore, having girded your waist with

TRUTH, having put on the breastplate of RIGHTOUSNESS, and having shod your feet with the preparation of the gospel of PEACE; above all, taking the shield of FAITH with which you will be able to quench all the fiery darts of the wicked one. And take the helmet of SALVATION and the sword of the spirit which is THE WORD OF GOD; praying always with all prayer and supplication in the spirit, being watchful to this end with all perseverance and supplication for all the saints.

Now let us look at the fighting side of these weapons as we go to war and retake the love one that war claims from us.

1. Be strong. Not in your power, because if you try that you will run out of gas in no time. Use Gods power and Gods might, that is our instruction in verse 10.

2. Recognize your enemy. See and know who your fight is really with, remembering it is not flesh and blood as verse 12 tells us, and be watchful. The devil doesn't care whose mouth he uses to hurt you and the closer you are to his mouthpiece the better. Because he will use words as venom to kill your heart and spirit in the battle. Keep in mind, he has claimed this mind as his prize but he has no right to it. So take it back!

3. Put on the WHOLE armor of God. When a fireman goes into the fire he is fully dressed for the task. All of his vitals are covered and protected from fatal injury. Therefore, we must be no less protected because the spiritual fires we fight are for the souls of men.

4. Use TRUTH in helping a wounded spirit, but make sure you use love when conveying the truth. TRUTH is a balm not a ball bat. When I would truthfully tell my husband things I always got a good reaction if I used a kind approach and not a defensive one. Sometimes the truth will hurt, but when given time to sink in and do its work, there will be a reward.

5. In using RIGHTEOUSNESS as a weapon, let us define it to aid us in its usage. The dictionary says it is ethical, chase, honorable, good, and virtuous. It is the opposite of being sinful, immoral, wrong and unfair. When our wounded loved one sees a behavior that cannot be criticized or judged, we can use this effective weapon to bring about the victory of wholeness for ourselves and those which we are influencing.

6. When we use PEACE it can be as a soothing ointment over a jagged wound. Keep in mind, it was the chaos of war and the visual horrors around them that has robbed them of the peace of mind they once had. Create a peaceful environment. Pray for the peace of their souls, speak peace as Jesus did when in Matthew 8:23-27 when he rebuked the winds and the sea and brought peace in a situation of turmoil. We can speak peace and cause the calm that is called for when we face a tempest in the spirit. Use it, it works. Walk away from the explosions of anger and fits of carnality brought on by the unsettled spirit of the man of war and rebuke the storm and speak PEACE.

7. FAITH - wow! The very definition is the help and hope we stand on, so let's look at it. In Hebrews 11:1 it says, "*Now faith is the substance of things hoped for, the evidence of things not seen.*" That is *now* faith, not later faith. Right now we are to hope because hope is the seed of faith. Whenever I wanted or needed to germinate faith I started by planting hope. I knew that by hoping I would create

believing and it would manifest to the result according to Gods word and his will. Don't make it so hard to believe in a loving and gracious Father, who desires wholeness of us all and paid the price for us to obtain it.

8. The armor of SALVATION will repel the despair and hopelessness which the enemy causes in those that have killed in battle. The forgiveness is the beginning element of wholeness. I always tell my children to forgive as quickly as possible because that's how fast I want God to forgive me. Jesus died to bring us salvation. The word salvation in the dictionary says it's a *release, a rescue and deliverance.* In the armor salvation is a helmet. It covers the mind which is the very target of the enemy to destroy us all. Pray for the salvation of your family. Receive Jesus as your Lord and Savior. Romans 10; 9 says, *"that if you confess with your mouth the Lord Jesus and believe in your heart that God has raised him from the dead, you will be saved."* God is not complicated. He doesn't make it too hard. We do. I'm going to use a simple but profound term to help you. "Let go and let God".

9. The most powerful weapon is THE WORD OF GOD. Learn it, repeat it, confess it, and believe it. Sometimes the devil needs to be reminded that he has already lost and that his judgment awaits him. Speaking the word of God has all the power to produce the victory for us. Have you ever told your children that you have the last word? Well God truly has the last word and we can depend on it. His word is life, truth, peace, salvation, strength, and

the light in the darkness. His word will comfort, affirm, lift up, heal all wounds and restore that which was lost. You must know the recipe before you can make the dish. You must have the key before you can start the engine. So you must learn the word of God to know him and what he has for you. Of this you must not slack or delay, but always study.

Now how do we protect ourselves as we wage war on our spiritual enemies? When you engage the enemy you must protect yourself. God has made provision with the same weapons we use to fight; we also use to protect ourselves. Let us explore once again the goodness of our heavenly Father as he has through his word provided us with the blueprint of victory. Let us take the armor one piece at a time and see the effectiveness of its usage. Verse 14 of chapter 6 in Ephesians gives us the first piece of armor

1. Gird your waist with truth. To "gird" means to surround or encircle as if a belt. Have you ever seen the employees of Wal-Mart use that black belt like waist band? Well, it supports their back and helps them to avoid injury. Truth supports our backs because if we injure our backs it impairs our walk. Truth is support. It holds us upright and straight. In the same way that those employees aid the support of their backs, truth aids us and supports us against injury. Without truth we couldn't walk too far.

2. The Breastplate of Righteousness is the second piece of armor we are given to ensure victory. A breastplate protects your heart. Right standing with God protects

our hearts from the fiery darts of the enemy. When we allow our hearts to go unprotected we risk fatal injury. When someone we love is under the attack of the enemy and uses words to wound us we must have on our breastplate in order to recognize the source of the attack. When we take our eyes off of the spiritual and begin to look at the natural, an explosion of emotions is bound to follow. When we do not protect ourselves we grow weary of well doing and we falter. If we do not stay the course, so much is lost. So beloved, protect your hearts with a chaste and godly lifestyle.

3. Weapon three is Peace, and what an insurance policy this is for us. We must give peace to our wounded. But we must first be able to receive it, and God has provided us a fountain of supply. In Isaiah 26; 3 it says, "*Thou wilt keep in perfect peace whose mind is stayed on thee; because he trusteth in thee*". Peace comes from trusting in God and Jesus is our true source of peace. He left it to us, it is part of our inheritance, and it is not corruptible like silver and gold but everlasting. In John 14; 27 Jesus said, "*Peace I leave with you, my peace I give unto you; not as the world giveth, give I unto you. Let not your heart be troubled, neither let it be afraid*". We must speak this peace to ourselves in the battle. Verse 15 says that we should shoe our feet with the preparation of peace. This describes for us that we must cover our walk and always be in the process of preparing the gospel of peace. Gospel means "good news" so are you prepared to speak peace and prepare peace in your situation? One thing that my husband truly

took notice of was the peace I had and how I faced the storm in peace. It causes others to want it, to so we must drink in the peace of God in order to dispense it to others.

4. THE SHIELD OF FAITH is a part of the armor that when used, causes such problems for the enemy. A shield protects from all directions as we move closer and closer in the battle. Have you ever watched the tactics in Roman warfare? They used their shields to make noise so that they could confuse the enemy about their numbers as they approached. They used them in formations to protect a whole group as well as the individual. They covered up in formation like a turtle and advanced on the battlefield. Faith is indeed our shield from the unseen enemy. Many passages in the Psalms state how God is our shield, read Psalms 91, Psalms 3:3, 28: 7, 33:20 and many more. Again, the shield like the breastplate protects the vital parts of the body from injury. Protection is God's expertise, and we will do well to stay under that protection. If we lose heart and if we are wounded by a lie of the enemy, God will defend us. All we have to do is pick up our shield and move forward. Remember God shoots arrows; the devil only has fiery darts.

5. In verse 17 it invites us to *"take the HELMET OF SALVATION"*. It is a simple deduction as to the use of a helmet isn't it? It protects our thoughts. Receiving salvation gives us a renewed outlook, a new found freedom from the oppression of our sins. If we do not

accept Christ as our Savior then we reject forgiveness and cleansing of our hearts, minds and spirits. Then what chance do we have? Without being born again we doom ourselves to a life of fiery darts constantly flying our way with no way of protecting ourselves, let alone being an instrument of God to help others. Renewing takes time. Remember how it seemed to take forever to rewind a cassette tape? Well that's what has to be done to renew our minds. We have to learn to think again without the clouded view that trauma can leave upon our souls, and the only way to find success is with God. If you haven't already done it, stop now, and pray and confess and believe Romans 10:9.

6. And now, the SWORD OF THE SPIRIT WHICH IS THE "WORD OF GOD". Last but not least as they say, with this sword our armor is complete. Let's see just how effective this sword is, shall we? In Hebrews 4:12 it says," *For the word of God is quick and powerful and sharper than any two-edged sword, piercing even to the dividing asunder of soul and spirit, and of the joints and marrow, and is a discerner of the thoughts and intents of the heart*". I like what the Message Bible says. It says" *Nothing and no one is impervious to God's word. We can't get away from it, no matter what*". It's sort of like "you can run but you can't hide". You must know the word of God and wield it as a sword to cut down every false accusation and lie of the enemy. He will tell you it's not worth it, or to give up because it's hopeless. But you must remember that there

> is no truth in him; he only knows how to lie and misrepresent the truth. By knowing God's word you have the power to overcome anything. Use the word to encourage yourself and strengthen your heart and mind in the troubled times. So, having done all to stand, stand therefore, because it works, it really does.

It is truly a shame upon our government that they never learned to put into place a program to de-program our men in war especially since war is ever on going in this world. Families are at risk, morals are at an all-time low and no one has any answers that make sense. While we waste away worrying about bills and jobs and how we are going to make it from week to week the answers are right before us. They have always been there and yet we seem so surprised when we finally see it. God is our ultimate help in time of trouble. He is the rock on which we can stand. All we have to do is chose to. Our warriors need us. Our children need to see the miracles of God and we as women can be just the conduit that God will use to bring it to pass. So, suit up ladies, put on your war paint, shout out your battle cry, this enemy is goin' down! Confess and believe with me:

My husband, Father, Brother, Uncle, or friend, will be whole again in Jesus Christ, He will no longer suffer the effects of war, but will have the mind of Christ in all things, he now possesses the peace of Jesus that passes all understanding, he no longer rages in his mind but he is whole. He is free in the name of Jesus.

Be at peace and fight a good fight, God will reward you.

PAT RAFFO

When my father's horse came in, he won a few thousand dollars. This meant we could finally get a house. My father picked an area around 38th and Post Road on the East side of Indianapolis and he built a house on Erickson Court. On the court, there were all new houses. Two houses down from us lived a couple named Don and Barb Cross. We moved into that house when I was around 14 years old. Don was much older than me and he had a long prison record that included seven years in Michigan City Prison. I didn't know at the time of our meeting. Now, Don was a bad dude. While in prison, he'd lifted weights all the time, so he was 240 pounds of muscle. He always had a nice car and at the time his wife was quite attractive. So I was intrigued by Don.

After I returned from Vietnam, I came home to find that my father gotten Don a job at the same factory he worked – The Schweitzer Corporation. But Don had his share of capers and was always involved in something, so he couldn't handle a straight job. He was always taking down scores or hustling something, so he didn't last long with Dad. Again like before, I was intrigued again and Don and I got closer. I was more mature, and after what I'd been through I could easily relate to Don. Don and I began hanging out often and I slowly began to learn how things operated inside and outside of the prison walls. That included keeping in touch with those who you'd done time with. Once you have a federal prison record, not too many people want to hire you, so the connections you made before could be beneficial to you afterwards - especially if you planned on continuing living a life of crime. While Don was in prison, he met a man named Pat Raffo, who was an older gentleman from New York City. Pat was always into something as well. So as I began spending more and more time at Don's house, various criminals would come by and hang out and scheme. These guys were always looking for the quick dollar and the fast hustle. They really didn't care since they had nothing else. Society had already chosen its opinions about them. Crime was all they had.

The first thing Don and I did together was absolutely crazy. You'd think if you were going to get into a life of crime you'd start out slowly; get your feet wet. Well not me! Don's brother in law got him a job at an auto dealership as night security, and he got brought me along with him. Our job was to walk the lot and make sure that everything was secure. Just basic lot security, if you will. We'd often sit in these new cars; we'd play cards and just chit chat. During the night, some of Don's contacts would slide by and hang out with us. Again, they were always scheming. They hatched an idea to steal some cars. So Don got the plan in motion by running copies of certain car keys. Our first automobile was a Ford camper. But it was a deluxe piece, so it was our target. Don's cohorts had ties to an auction house down in Alabama where they would wash the car. Somehow, you could take a stolen vehicle and wash it through the auction – I don't know all the particulars – and have yourself a new ride, free and clear. I'm not sure how long we did that, but we did several vehicles. Don decided he'd keep one for himself – a brand new Monte Carlo. We decided to take the Monte out to California.

We were tested immediately as we were passing through New Mexico and got stopped in the hot car. It had been washed through the Alabama auction, so this would be a true test. We were stopped for quite some time, so we were sweating. After the longest time, we were let go. Whew! So the plan worked and we quickly headed on out to California. We quickly left the car theft business and decided to go as straight as we could. But as far as stealing cars, I was done with that.

We sat down not long after that and decided we'd then go into the Import/Export business. We created a company called Main Floor Imports and based our operations out of Lawrence, Indiana. The thing that saved us in that town was a place called Aunt Bee's. She was really connected to the cops. Otherwise, we'd have been busted quickly. So she became a friend and looked out for us, since all kinds of riff raff were coming in and out of our store. Our business was primarily as a head shoppe.

We sold papers, hookah pipes, water bongs and pretty much anything that had to do with drug use. It was the 70's man!

We'd often go down to Mexico and drop 10 or 12k on things like leather goods, paintings, belts, purses, incense and anything that we thought were high-end, really nice pieces for our store. But we had to go deep into Mexico to get the merchandise. We could have purchased all our goods in Tijuana, but the goods there were low in quality. We wanted our merchandise to be top shelf at our store, so we took it to the next level and went further south into Ensenada, where we knew we could get the good stuff from a blond Mexican who was our contact there. We also had another contact that was high up in the Navy who helped us get things duty free and over the border easier. So starting out, we had a great line of contacts and people who were in the know.

We came back to Indiana and filled up our store with the things we'd shipped from California. For added dinero, Don of course was still scheming on the side. He got in touch with a guy out of New York named Pat Raffo, a guy he'd done time with in Michigan City. I never knew what Pat's past was and I didn't want to know. But he had to have done something pretty bad to have done a long stint in Michigan City. Pat had a nice little racket he was running up there involving clothing and all other kinds of trinkets and various merchandise. The plan was to go to New York and set up a little network and get some high quality clothing to add to the store's inventory. We figured if we had some clothing from California and New York, we'd be ahead of the curve. Well, Pat could get us the kind of things we were looking for. Problem is he wanted something in return. Like moving his stolen goods. Don and Pat were close, and soon after, Pat allowed me into the operation on Don's word.

Main Floor Imports had a lot of convicts running in and out of the store. We were hot from the jump due to what we were selling. So we kept our noses as clean as we could, but the narcs were in and out of there, looking for us to slip up. We were often close to doing just that due to the high number of stolen goods we were filling up our store with. The guys from New York would bring the goods to us and we'd fill up the store. We had such a hodge-podge of stuff in there. From flashlights to garbage disposals, anything you could think of, if Pat could get it, we tried to move it. Pat had a big front up there in Brooklyn, as he owned a drug store. So Pat had stuff moving everywhere. He was huge with money coming every which way. To say Pat was connected is an understatement. I didn't know and I didn't want to know.

We had a contact there that had some inside information and a scheme on rail cars that carried cigarettes. Pat was interested in cigarettes of course, for his drug store and his bar contacts. The danger for us was if we broke a federal seal on the railroad car or a semi truck, we were in deep. So we had to be extremely careful and always worked it from the inside. But our guy had a pistol just in case. My job was just to haul the goods out. So Don and I, along with our network of convicts worked the docks and rails all the time, looking to steal and hijack. And these guys were the best, and Pat could move all of it. He was always the point man.

Pat set us up with an apartment in Brooklyn not long after and every morning we'd head out to lower Manhattan to work the street carts. We'd work them three times a day and in the meantime, we'd go shopping for sources for Main Floor Imports. As far as moving the stolen goods for Pat, we'd get up there before rush hour before everyone started work. The trucks would pull into the alleys or in between the buildings and we'd start loading the merchandise on the carts. As long as we were moving, we could do it. The store owners didn't like it, so sometimes we'd get arrested to make it look legit. But Pat had his contacts in the police force, so it would be an in and out deal. This was done just to appease the store owners. It was just a game. We knew the game and that's just how it was played. I didn't ask too many questions. I just did what I was supposed to. About every two weeks or so, we'd all meet up at an Italian restaurant and Pat would pass out the envelopes to everyone, police included. It was straight out of The Godfather. Pat seemed to have everyone on pocket.

We worked for Pat about a year or so. One day, I just decided I didn't want to do it anymore. The money was good and things were going great, but it just hit me one day and I told Don I was out. Don thought I was kidding, because things were rolling big time for us, but I wasn't. It was just the way I was made at the time. I got sick of it and wanted to move on. Don was trying to convey to me that you just don't quit working for Pat Raffo, but I didn't care. I told him to handle it and that I was out. I was done. Pat didn't own me and I was going to do what I wanted to do. Don had to have done something or cleared it up with

Pat, because that was the end of it for me, and I never heard from or dealt with Pat again. The connections and ties that Pat had could have come back to bite me. I could have been an open ended leak that Pat needed to patch up eventually. But again, the Edge was there for me. Back in Indy, the pressure to close the head shoppe from the locals and the heat from the cops just got too much, and we had to shut it down.

Not long after, I met up with an old friend named Skip who had partnered up with a guy named Royce Spears. Skip wanted to build a state of the art recording studio on the south side of Indianapolis and needed partners. Royce was a big time home builder who really loved Bobby Goldsboro, who was a famous country singer at the time. Royce even had a custom built guitar made for Goldsboro, so having Royce build and fund the studio was a good fit. Royce always wanted to be a comedian, so the plan was to have Royce back most of it and he'd get as much studio time as he wanted to help fulfill his dream of standup comedy. So I put in about ten grand of my money to become a partner and was back on the road to legitimacy. The studio was the best in the business. We had it all decked out with all the best gear. Royce even went out and bought Paul McCartney's mellotron to put in the studio. We picked up the best engineer we could find; a guy named John Lazott, who eventually went on to be a big time jazz engineer in Indianapolis. We had it all – the drum room, the gear, the grand piano, you name it. We spent a fortune to get this studio in top shape. We called it Dove Recording, and we picked up all the big bands in the local area. We were doing well.

Things were going well and then someone, I don't know who, decided to bring in, along with the scores of women and booze that were moving in and out of there - coke. Well, that was the end of it for all of us. I got addicted immediately. It gripped me and I was in trouble. I knew right away I was in deep. We were doing it almost nonstop. I was at the point where I my habit was at $1000 a week. I was using bad and losing weight – full blown addicted. But for some reason, I loved it. It was the drug for me. None of the drugs I had ever done up to that point had done much for me, but coke was the king. I knew it was going to kill me eventually, but I didn't care.

It was during that time that Skip told me about a program called "The Way", which would really change my life in a way that I could never imagine.

TWO GODS, TWO DESTINATIONS

The one true God and Satan (the God of this world) – that statement made a lot of sense to me and to others wondering why there was so much grief and misery in this world. I often wondered why if there was an all powerful God, why would he not step in. The answer to that is the gospel, which shows that he does step in. He did so once by sending his son to die for the sins of the world. The guy that told me about the two Gods was brand new to the faith and was armed with only enough information to make him dangerous. It didn't help that his doctor had come from "The Way". Later I would find out that it wasn't the true way, but a cult.

Out of all the churches in America, what are the odds that my first introductions to religion would be a cult that was spawned from hell? I don't know genuine from counterfeit at this point. The first thing that made sense was that Satan was tearing things up and destroying things. I immediately flashed back to the war in Vietnam, so it made a bit of sense. The founder of the cult was Dr. Victor Paul Wierwille. He was pretty much out there in terms of doctrine and beliefs. One of the things that stood out for me was that he smoked as he taught from the word of God. He wasn't on fire with any anointing – he smoked cigarettes. The structure of the cult involved small cell meetings all over the country. Meetings were in homes and called "Twig Meetings".

They had a Twig leader who would answer to a Branch leader, which was a higher tier in the system.

They say that ignorance is no excuse for the law. Well, I had "stupid" written all over me. The Way had the "look" and the devil made sure of it. If you're going to have a counterfeit, it needs to look legit, just like the apple that enticed Adam and Eve. It looked good on the outside, but after one bite, you're in trouble.

On the front end or the "enticement phase" were the Twig meetings, where afterwards we would smoke pot and partied when we finished hearing the word of God. Things looked real good to me. There was an atmosphere of no condemnation and I liked that. It meant I wouldn't have to change my lifestyle at all. Now here's what sealed the deal for me – They Way had a nice college in Kansas and the campus reflected the air that was prevalent. They had free and open sex on campus and marijuana smoking was widely accepted in the group. As we were pulling into the campus after a long drive from Indiana, there was a pond in the front where many young people were swimming. Just as we pulled in, their nude bodies were coming out of the water. As soon as I saw that, I knew I was in. In that moment I knew I was going to join. Where do I sign up? I guess I didn't learn much from my time working for Uncle Sam. Face value had me sucked in. At the time, I had a big cocaine habit. So far, it looked like I was going to be accepted anyway. Satan's door is always open wide until he's done with you.

We wrapped up our trip in Kansas, and I did all I needed to do to know whether or not I was in or out. There was nothing negative about The Way at first glance, but underneath that there was mass deception and fraud. But at the time, what do I know? I was looking for answers at the time, and this organization provided them with their love and acceptance. Somebody threw a net on top of all of us! I truly wasn't in my right mind (again).

The next step in the enrollment process involved paying $100 for ten to twelve segments of teachings. The final session was the big one. They had promised that after the big session, everyone would receive the Holy Ghost. They made it out to be a huge event – and it truly is - but not from the counterfeit. I paid my $100, and I was definitely in. There was certainly a tremendous amount of digging into the word of God; however it left me with more questions than answers. I was more dangerous than ever, because I'm in a cult and I don't know it. At the end of each session, the smoking light came on – or whatever addictions gripped you – coke, alcohol, pot, speed and so forth. Let the party begin! Church was good! I sure had come a long way from "God Help Me". Sin was prevalent, and deep down I knew it. Reading and studying the word brought both conviction and confusion. It took me right back to the confusion I felt during the war - seeking for answers but only being led down trails that led to more questions.

Soon the final session arrived and anticipation was in the air. I had this excitement that something big was going to happen to me that night. It was during this final meeting that I did what I was instructed and accepted Christ into my life. But it was more than just words. Now my heart was struck with a reality of God and what Jesus did for me. I was so convicted and really wanted to change. I wanted to feel the freedom from the phantoms that haunted me and condemned me for the killings during the war. I wanted set free from the sins of crime that I so easily involved myself with. I entered into the full "hope" mode when it came to receiving the Holy Spirit, because it would give me a new beginning and a new spiritual life. I wanted that desperately.

Now in this group of twenty or so people, we're all reciting the prayer of invitation of receiving the Holy Spirit. The room was electric, as one by one each person started to break out in tongues. But me, nothing. Nothing was happening at all. Everyone else is over the top with joy, muttering in tongues. But I had nothing happening. I felt nothing. Looking back, I don't know what they were speaking, but God had determined for me that it wasn't going to take place here - not at this time. I didn't know that at the time, because at this point I'm sticking out like a sore thumb.

I'm devastated inside and wondering what is wrong with me. I'm the only one. Soon, everyone is looking at me like something's wrong. So some of the senior members decided to take me upstairs and work on me there. I never really looked at the possibility of not receiving the spirit, as no one ever said it wasn't a possibility. I knew there was something wrong with me, because I wasn't functioning like everyone else. I was broken, a reject, yet again. Wow, don't it figure? Many things are racing through my mind. I kept looking back at the things I had done. The enemy was telling me, "You really don't think you were going to get second chance, did you? After all you've done?" Finally after trying and trying, the senior members gave up. They told me they couldn't help me. But I pressed them further. I was desperate. I had to get the Holy Spirit! I knew hell was a real place, filled with horror and demons and I didn't want to go there. I was visibly shaken. I begged them to continue to try to help me. Then their cold, chilling words took me to a new level of doom and gloom.

"You are born again of the wrong seed."

That meant that I was a child of Satan. I was going to hell and there was no way to stop it. Talk about a dream killer; a destiny stopper. Hopelessness hit me. But thank God, Jesus is the way, the truth and the life. I did not flip to that truth at the time. There was nothing left for me there; no reason to stick around to celebrate with the dandelion wine and pot. I had to get out and my first order of business was finding an exit to get out of that place immediately. I was devastated and immediately began replaying the sins I had committed in my mind. I deserved this fate. I felt hopeless, and it seemed it all stacked up and made sense. The pressure and oppression on me then made me want to say when someone complained about a bad day – "Shut up! Try this one – I'm born again of the wrong seed and a child of the devil. I'm going to hell. How's that for a bad day?"

My future was nonexistent. I would have killed myself, but I wasn't ready to embrace going to hell just quite yet. I was too weak. As I'm driving home that night, I was physically sick. Despair doesn't even come close to explaining what I was feeling that night. Everlasting torment. This is beyond a death sentence. I was overwhelmed with depression for about two weeks. I simply shut myself away from everyone. Then one evening as I lay awake in bed, basically wallowing in self pity, I felt prompted in the midst of it to try one more time. I grabbed my bible and took myself through salvation. I wept and repented before the Lord with all my heart. As I gained strength through my repentance, I began to confess that I was not born again of the wrong seed. I was not a child of Satan. I was a child of God and I belonged to him. I continually spoke those things and confessed that Jesus was my lord and savior. I got radical about it and I began to believe what I was saying. I decided to go a step further and ask for the baptism of the Holy Spirit. I wanted to speak in tongues and I wanted freedom from my life of drug addiction. As I was praying, I was slain in the spirit. I fell on my bed and began speaking in an unknown tongue. A light entered my room that was blinding, and there was a flow that burst out of me that is beyond description. God seized the moment and totally delivered me from cocaine and everything else I was addicted to.

My mind had not been so clear in so long. I was totally set free. God touched my mind and a fog lifted. I spoke in tongues for days. I got into the spirit every chance I had. Many times it was just to see if I still had it. I know it was silly and I didn't have to do it. Every time I would see someone from The Way, I would display my gift by speaking in tongues and would tell them, "See, I'm not a child of the devil!" God soon stopped me and impressed upon my spirit that I didn't need to do that. I had the real thing. I knew my next step was to break away from everyone affiliated with The Way and everyone in my circle of drug dealing and crime.

I thought I needed a change of scenery and a new start. So I packed up to move to Florida. On my way, I felt conviction during the whole trip. But I kept going. The whole trip eventually became fruitless, as everything I attempted to do backfired and went wrong. The reason why everything went wrong was because at the same time this was going on, God was putting a Godly woman in front of me; a woman who knew the word, was well-grounded and had exactly what I needed. Prior to going to Florida, I had just met her, and there was something very special about her. That something special was Jesus Christ in her and all the gifts and talents he had given her. She would soon become my wife. Through the years I keep finding out that my plans were not God's plans, and looking back, I am so glad for that. I'm still learning that one. I'm relearning these lessons and have become very good at that. At least the time I spend going around the barn is getting shorter.

Proverbs 18:22-23: "He who finds a wife finds a good thing and attains favor from the Lord. "

My sister introduced Jackie to me before I left for Florida. As I said before, there was something special about her that I was attracted to beyond just physical appearance. She was peaceful even though she had been through a painful divorce and was raising her children alone. I had never been married because I was so goofed up from Vietnam and could not stay in a relationship very long. Jackie was very well grounded in the Lord. She knew the word of God and wasn't afraid to use it. I was so hungry for God but I knew nothing. When I got back from Florida, I would call her and we would talk for hours about scriptures and the truths of God. She wasn't interested in a relationship and neither was I. Besides, she had children and that looked like a lot of responsibility to me. Here is proof again that our plans are empty and God's are full of purpose.

We began to spend more time together, going out to dinner as well as time on the phone. It didn't take long and we found ourselves in love. In spite of the obstacles, I felt that I could trust Jackie because the Vietnam War had sadly touched her family as well.

Most of her friends were veterans and her brother in law had been killed there. She was very understanding and compassionate about the war and the problems veterans had coming home. God was answering my prayers and adding a bonus, which was giving me the desires of my heart - and that was having a wife and children. I was so attracted to her and I felt safe in the relationship. God so completely knows what we want and need. I bless him for his foreknowledge in my life. Jackie and I were married and I must say she is the best thing (besides Jesus) that has ever happened to me. I have tested and tried this woman like you would not believe. But she has stuck it out with me for many years. Jackie and I nave nine children all together and words fail me after saying that.

It's been a journey. Finding a help mate is not something we ourselves should tackle.

This kind of selection should be handled by God, who knows what we really need.

Jackie and I have always prayed for the right mates for our children and grandchildren. The value of a good wife or husband is immeasurable. God found me a good one in

Jackie.

God's purpose and destiny began with three words:

"God, Help Me!"

TASTE OF DEATH – GET YOUR FILL OF SOUL FOOD

As war heats up and long before the smell of death dominates inferior aromas belching from the terrain, attempting to inject lethal munitions and chemicals that kill for generations, hidden agendas, treachery, betrayal and greed are some of the players who prepare the secret banquet. The war will be in full swing and it will be too late as some of the pieces fit together and come to light. Deception always blinds the minds that matter, and the truth and what's right get lost as war burns hot within the soul.

Has anyone ever noticed that war never seems to be what it's supposed to be? There is so much to say here, however I will leave that trail for someone else. One statement I will make is, it's beyond sad and a disgrace that so many paid a steep price not really knowing or given the truth or how the deal of war is cut. In wrapping up God Help Me, I wanted to drive some points home and challenge all those affected by war.

I had my taste of death and my fill of soul food. Hopefully this book will cause a stir and moreover a firestorm that will open the door to lessons learned. I don't know about you, but I become furious when I see epidemic numbers of homeless veterans and PTSD off the charts - it goes back to lessons learned, or more importantly, not learned.

I was sent to a war zone in Vietnam and my first day was the full meal deal. My stomach was not ready for it. It's like back in the world, it takes time to adjust to foreign food. But it was a forced meal situation. Many can't take the food of war and they don't like the taste. Some like it hot and others do not. But there is one constant; there are plenty of leftovers. The Vietnam vet was programmed with an aggressive kill mindset with a high expectation and focus that we would eat Charlie's lunch and dinner and soon be home for breakfast. In every war, those who decide war and make decisions have never tasted death or smelled its smell. War must be seen all the war through. We must have an "all the way" attitude and think it through. The last things a soldier need are people with no backbone who won't see it all the way to the end. A combat soldier doesn't know how to back peddle. It's one gear - move forward, take the hill, advance and take no prisoners.

In 1969 Vietnam, after getting bogged down in this war due to wishy-washy, mamby-pamby limp-wristed politicians who wanted to compromise, Hanoi wanted victory. When you commit lives to war, you need decisive decision makers and military strategists who have the tasted death. Because anyone who was in combat has it. I want someone who has had their fill of soul food. The obvious reason is, they will be the last to commit our nation's youth unless we're in it to win it and the cause lines up with who we are. Not for the few operating in the shadows. In Vietnam, we were told to stay hungry for war Most of us thought we had a full appetite for it and could digest anything in front of us. The truth is our system wasn't ready for everything the war was serving up. Our system was used to a steady diet of American cuisine. But war food comes with pain and misery and the smell is like none other. Each portion is hard to swallow and there is an adjustment period your system needs for it to be able to handle the unfamiliar foreign soul food.

Remember war always seems to take a wrong turn after the war mongers and profiteers have sucked the money out of the war investment. The timing and change of atmosphere consistently comes part way through the course of each war. Regret sets in for many politicians that are heavily influenced or funded by war profiteers. Their munitions stocks have played out and are now flat. However the takeout is already in their accounts and now it's time to lobby for an exit strategy. It's the same crowd we see in the mortgage meltdown. Prior to the collapse, the smart money people were pitching toxic mortgages to their investors while holding a secret short position on that same investment. These people are criminals, and you'll now find them over and over in Iraq. When we didi mau, they will be going long in companies like "Baghdad

Doors", that tout, "Our doors will withstand the kickin' but not the tickin'". Our guys kicked in every door in that country, so the market for doors is huge and the profiteers are waiting.

In Vietnam there were many who would dine and dash and defect after they realized what they tasted could kill them. They concluded that the cost was too high. The exit or easy road was in front of all of us. Let's just stiff those who left us with this lousy experiment. Many in our country never made it even close to the fixings of war as they chose another course in Canada or elsewhere. What made it easier during the Vietnam War was that our country was divided at every level. Those who did their job and served their country were rejected and in some cases were condemned. Some of us were even assigned to hunt down these defectors. Wow, what a mind screw. This helps you get your fill of soul food.

To recap, the universal smell of death dominates and overpowers what's cooking in the war zone. The stench of death becomes less repulsive when the other soldier dies for his country, they are stinking up the terrain and the maggots are full of VC carcasses. When people read this, I want them to become sickened by war, because what it really comes down to is this; there are only a few reasons to ever go to war, and it's most obvious so I won't write them down. To further hammer this down, the tab of war in dollars and cents is paid by all of us via taxes. The real tab of war is paid in buckets of blood and more. This flesh and blood war touches the families of these warriors - sons, daughters, husbands and wives and even extends deeper to friends.

The soul food is shared among all and affects all. The taste of death remains.

War opens the door to treachery, betrayal and sometimes your dinner mates – those close in your ranks – are plotting to take you out. I know firsthand what that feels like. Jesus knew all about treachery and betrayal and it can be read in God's word at the last supper, as Judas betrayed the most innocent man who ever walked the face of the earth.

A war or cause will bring out the worst and best. Just when you've had your fill of soul food and you can't stand another bite, you rotate out. You find yourself home and everyone has these elaborate dinner plans for you. It's not their fault. They don't know the warrior who's coming home to dinner. In fact, the soldier himself doesn't know. At face value, it seems harmless and it's what people do. It's what the soldier used to do, but something now is off. The combat vet is full and ready to explode. But you can't let anything out because what you've done and been through is not fit for any dinner conversation. In fact, it's really best left alone because the combat vet is a pressure cooker. The pressure must be released a little at a time. There is usually much inside. I don't have any simple formula for release. Each case and soldier is different. What each soldier has engaged in and seen and done is difficult to measure. Your mind and soul have protection mechanisms. The complexities and scope of what each soldier faced is layered one bite of war at a time.

This goes back to how many "clicks", as the book comes to an end, until the convergence of this content reaches its destination. Life on this planet is about movement; the steps we take and the choices we make and others who may make them for us. I like to break it down in life's clicks. How many clicks until the final outcome? I don't know. Only God knows, and he has been known to extend lives. The big question for all of us is "How many clicks do you have in your mission in life?"

In the jungle, each mission was measured in "clicks" - one thousand yard pieces at a time. All the squad leaders were called to the Command Post, which was normally located in the middle of the 360. As I return to my squad before we can even relax for a second, the number of clicks was on everyone's mind. A lot of it had to do with all the humping we'd done earlier in the day. Before you could rest, you had to set up your kill zone and perimeter, because Charlie was always watching. He liked to attack before we set up; because he knew we were always tired and worn out from humping all day. This was when we were most vulnerable. With very few clicks left, sometimes it's just a barrage of mortars and rockets, but it was effective. Charlie also knew how long it took to lock into his position and call in fire support. It didn't change the mission, it only confirmed what we knew – the enemy was out there.

Again, life is about movement. As we progress and move forward on our designed and unique path and advance in the clicks in life, there is a dual tracking on your movement. We all have a real enemy out there named Satan. With him, his dark forces have been assigned both general and specific orders for those who have a higher threat level. The standing general order is to take each one of us out. That is, unless you are a temporary help to the kingdom of darkness. Eventually when you're of no use anymore, it's automatic. David Koresh and his cult followers are a prime example of a cult figure whose sphere of influence brought down many people. Hitler, Pol Pot, Mao Tse Tung, Lenin, Stalin, Saddam Hussein, Idi Amin and many others have taken out huge numbers because their wills aligned with Satan and his agenda. As this book draws to a close, it's important to put into perspective the two realms that are at play as we live and move in this world.

The breakdown is like this in the jungle – as we were fighting in the natural realm, our enemy was called Charlie, and both sides had a war agenda, and that was to take the other out. At the same time, in the invisible realm or the supernatural, the action was just as real. However it was an unseen realm. The angels and demons battle and each has orders and assignments. We were engaged full in a flesh and blood fight. The spiritual fight is more complex due to who you belong to, intercessory prayer, callings, destinies, purpose and so much more. I have said this before and I'll say it again. My shout out to God was a defining moment; a turning point for me. This faith action saved my soul and my life. It's been said, only faith can cause you to arrive at your destination. On that war-ravaged hill, three words of faith – "God Help Me" – put me in an eternal position in a split second; from a pagan going to hell to a Son going to heaven. His faithfulness is exciting, as we move one click after another. Yes, trouble will arrive in war or anywhere on the planet. When it rises up, speak the word. Philippians 4:13 in the message bible reads:

Whatever I have, wherever I am, I can make it through anything in the One who makes me who I am.

These are words of life, not death. Knowing that you have a destiny and seeing that destiny ahead will keep a focus in your life. So when we fall, we can get back up and press on. Destiny calls you. You can run but you can't hide. So become what you believe. Yes, in this world your enemies are sprouting like mushrooms. Remember, God is bigger than anything you face.

I am speaking to warriors and freedom fighters. I am trying to give you everything I can and pour into you, because I've been where you are. I still have to fight every day to keep the victory and ground I've taken. This would be just another book without God's anointing and grace on it. Remember, with those you face about war's events and all the trauma that comes along with it - a man with an argument is no match for a man with experience. My experience was very unique because of the mix of supernatural and God's divine intervention. Those who want to argue can write their own book! Remember the dual tracks - two realms. In the invisible, the enemy seeks to destroy faith and produce doubt. He seeks to destroy hope and produce despair. He seeks to destroy humility and produce pride. He seeks to destroy peace and produce bitterness and malice.

The attack, my brothers and sisters, will be on the soul and the mind. So renew your mind! My friends, we are living in what's called "The End Times". The last big movement will be spiritual warfare. The key is specialists, just like in the Nam. War, what is it good for? Absolutely everything in the spiritual realm! There are a lot of doomsday scenarios out there. But remember, it's over when God says it's over. War is chaos, but in the midst of chaos, there is opportunity. I wanted to take this opportunity to tell you that the taste of war and all the traumatic events that come along with it will no longer have a hold on you. The soul food you need is the word of God. The freedom you are looking for can be found along this path – Romans 10:9:

That if you confess with your mouth the Lord Jesus and believe in your heart that God

has raised Him from the dead, you will be saved.

Now, know this – Jesus sealed the deal. Believe in your heart that God raised Jesus from the dead and receive your new heart. Receive your new mind. Receive your new identity change. The key is, "Jesus I need you. Forgive me of my sins. I'm giving you my life. I believe you died, were buried and rose again on the third day. I'm expecting a new destiny and new life. I now call you Savior. In Jesus' name. "

THE JOURNEY OF GOD HELP ME

A man recently asked an author, "How do you write a book?" After a long pause, the author replied, "You sit down and write." As basic as that response was, truer words have never been spoken with it comes to writing.

Helping Steve with writing *God Help Me* has been quite a journey, both emotionally and mentally. My fingers did more walking than the Yellow Pages. From the beginning until now, I have experienced a wide range of emotions; from encouragement, joy, relief and discovery to confusion, frustration, anger and rage.

Steve began the basis for *God Help Me* in the mid 90's, forming a series of thoughts and placing them down on paper. In talking to him, it was more of a therapy session for him rather than looking further into the future at the big picture. Even then, when Steve let people read what he had written, they couldn't put it down. Then, life took over and the book took a back seat. We resurrected it in the summer of 2003 and started a journey to what has culminated into what you're holding in your hands right now. Let me tell you, it hasn't been easy, because in 2005, life took over again and the book rested on a shelf. In the meantime though, I told Steve that I would begin searching for some of his old platoon-mates. When I began my search, I spoke with a young lady named Jeannie (the wife of a Vietnam Vet who has since passed) who worked at the census bureau. She was so kind and was able to mail me several company rosters from that time. I found Steve's name along with a few of his other friends. Thank you for your help Jeannie!

But the battle for concrete records had just begun, and it was to be a nightmare. I just didn't know it yet. I'll elaborate on that in a moment.

In the fall of 2010, we made a decision to get the book finished and published. We took what Steve had started to write in the 90's and cherry picked what we would keep and what we would discard. We made a commitment to meet every Thursday at 6pm and write the book. I would bring my trusty little recording device and a bag or two of some good coffee and we would sit and talk. Sometimes our discussions lasted but an hour. Other times, as long as three. But we seldom missed a Thursday night meeting.

Our plan was to encompass not only the tour in Vietnam, but to address pre and post war. Our planning was a little more solid than the war mongers. That meant delving into Steve's childhood prior to 1968 and after the war with PTSD, his Agent Orange and health afflictions and battle with the V.A. We both knew this meant that spiritual attacks would come and come swiftly; and they did. But we never wavered from the task at hand, and that was putting together a true edge-of-your-seat thrill ride.

Throughout the journey, for me personally, I encountered road block after road block. I began searching for Steve's close friends Junior and Larry in 2005. I scoured the internet. I scoured people searches. I scoured libraries. I called the Marine Corps and filed papers with the V.A. I got nowhere with Junior. I gave up there for a while, and then in the fall of 2010 I started the search again. Larry, I found quickly and put him in touch with Steve, where they talked for a while and caught up. It was good to see Steve so happy to be talking to one of his old buddies; and an old buddy who confirmed quite a bit of what we've added to this book. In regards to Junior, by pure chance, I was able to use an address on a Christmas card Junior sent in 1971 and find his spouse's name. From there, I cross referenced possible high schools in the area and finally stumbled upon a reunion site, where I found her. After emailing her about Junior's whereabouts, we found out that he had been killed in 1993. I toiled with that information for two days, wondering how I would tell Steve. For some reason, even though it had been over forty years since they'd last spoke, we both just knew we would find him. We did. Unfortunately it was not the way we wanted to. I knew he would be crushed, but I finally sat down and told Steve at our next meeting. I could tell he was devastated, but he didn't show it. Later, he told me that it was because of the war and the *don't mean nothin'* factor that all Nam vets would say when they lost a friend in country. He was just numb to it. Fortunately though, Steve and Junior's widow and daughter have begun corresponding and I want to thank her for being so gracious in our search and for answering my many questions.

Searching for records, now that was an entirely different and even more difficult battle. I had many of Steve's Vietnam paperwork in hand, as he keeps impeccable records. I had his DD-214 (which was blank in several vital areas), his Navy Commendation Medal and several other pieces of information on hand. The unit diaries I had were now lost, as I had moved twice since 2003. So now, I needed to go back to the drawing board to get those in my hands again. I reached out to the V.A. and requested the unit diaries. I was sent some forms in the mail (after weeks of waiting) that told me to go to another place. The same thing happened there. It wasn't until I searched the National Archives where I was able to pinpoint the building, row and actual box where the records were stored that someone finally helped me. A few weeks later, I got the unit diaries and company rosters and I could barely read them since they'd been photocopied multiple times over. Here is the National Archive and they don't even have an original? But none the less, the documents were valuable and I was able to get names we were looking for and dates. Emotions one and two - encouragement and joy....Check.

As we continued with the interview process every Thursday, I noticed that Steve's memory with certain events was fragmented. He'd remember who was with him on a certain day, but couldn't remember the village or hamlet name. He could remember certain mission details, but couldn't remember whether he was in the Ashau or up near the DMZ. I've learned since then that this is a common occurrence with Veterans who have PTSD. What they wish to remember they can't, and what they wish to forget is forever burned in the front of their minds. So, I set out to piece together a timeline of Steve's tour and attempt to get as much information about these missions in order to finally bring together and fully restore Steve's memory. It was a simple goal in my mind. I wanted to be able to sit down with a map of North Vietnam and trace from the time Steve landed on that hot LZ until he left the service and went to Yokosuka. Easy enough, right? I scoured military sites, trying to map up the time line with specific missions that took place during his time. Slowly the puzzle pieces began coming together.

I went to several Vietnam veteran websites online and reached out. I explained who I was and specifically asked if anyone knew (1) a couple of Steve's old buddies and (2) if anyone could add some input and insight to the missions I was asking for. Basically, "Hey, if you were there, I'd love to hear your story". I figured if I could get a few viewpoints from guys who were on some of these missions too, I could help Steve regain the memories he'd lost there. I specifically asked for guys who were there at "The River" and the Pacification program. I also wanted to know more about "Special Projects". Asking those questions - what a can of worms did they open.

Being that Steve was a member of Hotel 2/3/3 - Charlie Company, I figured some of those guys who be eager to talk and perhaps even want to get back in touch with Steve. Was I ever wrong! For one, their memories were just as fragmented. Secondly, and as Steve had told me before, many of these guys ran in tight groups over there. Since there were so many fighting in Vietnam, once you had a core group of buddies there, you didn't really mingle with others outside your core group. As I began to ask questions to some of these veterans, responses ran the gamut from one end of the spectrum to the other. Emotion Numbers five and six – confusion and frustration. Check.

One veteran I spoke to (and from here on out, all names will be anonymous to protect the guilty) told me straight, "If you release this book, I will do everything in my power to discredit you." This came right out of left field, as I hadn't even gone into any details of the book. I just wanted information, and possibly help to put the mission details together. He would give me none. I remember him being very angry, cursing at me and asking why I would want to write a book about their time over there. He told me I should leave things well enough alone. In the middle of the conversation, his tone suddenly changed. Eerily, in fact. It was as though he passed the phone to someone else. Ironically, he then asked me if Steve and I would be attending the reunion that year. In the words of Jacob McCandles, I replied, "Not hardly."

The second set of veterans I spoke to really blew the doors of secrecy, cover-ups and lies wide open. It was as though a light shone down from heaven with the tune from Handel's Messiah ringing out loud.

I was able to track down the son of a Veteran who was an integral part in Steve's tour. I emailed him, explaining the details of my request and asking if I could interview his father for the book. Two weeks passed with no response. Then out of the blue, a phone call. It was like the Spanish Inquisition. Why was I emailing? What did I want? Who was I? I politely answered all questions and he told me his father would get back to me. A month passed and finally an email response this time, with more questions which I answered yet again. Two months passed. Then I got the phone call from the Veteran himself. He was very friendly, but closed off. He didn't remember Steve specifically, but did remember certain instances. I asked him about Special Projects. I asked him about missions. I asked him what he did after the war and if he had PSTD (yes) and Agent Orange poisoning (no). I was honest. He confirmed my suspicions about Special Projects (and CIA involvement) and told me a little about what he did over there, but was very ambiguous in his responses. He was hiding something. I knew it. And he knew that I knew it. I left the conversation asking even more questions.

A couple of months later, I received two emails from two veterans who claimed they were at the river and wanted to know more about Steve. I was cautious due to my earlier conversation, but optimistic because they both confirmed a few pertinent details.

The first veteran was completely open with me regarding covert ops and cover-ups.

When I asked him if he'd ever heard of Special Projects, he replied, "*Oh yeah. Worst of*

the worst. Those were the real expendables over there. They hand-picked grunts who they knew wouldn't be missed if they were killed." He went on to explain to me that Special Projects contracted out a handful of grunts from different companies for special missions in North Vietnam, Laos and Cambodia. These small four to five man teams would face missions such as assassinations, long range recon, capturing enemies for interrogation and defector termination. He stated that it was under the Phoenix Program banner and advised me to research that. When I explained the story of The River to him, he wasn't shocked that Steve received the Navy Commendation Medal and others received Bronze Stars and other higher ranked awards that day – for performing the same acts of bravery.

He said, "*Ask yourself this. Why would the government give a high ranking award to a grunt who's doing dirt behind the scenes? When you get major medals like that, it puts you in the spotlight, out in front of the world. They had to give Steve something, because someone documented it. But I believe that when they realized who Steve was, they gave him the lowest award they could to save face. But there's no way they're gonna give a major award to a guy in Special Projects. Why, so he can tell the world what he's been doing under the cover of darkness? The fact that he got shot the next day and still hasn't received a Purple Heart tells me all I need to know."*

I came back to Steve with this information and laid it all out that night. I thought Steve would be relieved to receive such information, but instead he began to sob. As if his family life and childhood didn't spawn enough rejection, he entered the Marine Corps voluntarily hoping that they'd accept him as a fighting and killing machine. Instead, they decided that he was expendable, and placed him in a group that they fully expected wouldn't make it back home. It all hit me at once as I watched him cry. It broke my heart.

Steve had never heard of the Phoenix Program, so I researched it. The missions performed under the Phoenix banner were just as Steve had described to me throughout the book writing process. Missions he told me about (that are not in this book) were almost scary specific as to what Phoenix's plan entailed. The CIA ran it for a while and contracted out assassinations, torture, you name it. It was also done under the guise of Pacification, which gave me more confirmation of Steve's time in Quang Tri and other various missions he told me about. Not long after, the CIA passed off the program to MACV, and they closed it down shortly after. Bottom line, Special Projects was run by the CIA, and Steve was a part of it.

The second veteran really became a thorn in my side, and became one very quickly. He started off very kind and answered all my questions, giving me a very detailed account of his view of the events at the river, even confirming to me that the Operation was in fact, Dewey Canyon as we suspected. He mentioned other vets specifically by name, even going as far as telling me that one of Steve's friends who he thought was killed that day actually lived. Steve was shocked at the news; almost in a state of disbelief, for he knew he'd been killed because he saw him get shot multiple times. Not so said the man. He was in fact alive, paralyzed from the neck down due to the events of that day. In fact, no one in the platoon knew he lived for close to twenty years. He was medevaced out so quickly and discreetly that even his close friends thought he'd died as well.

Emotion numbers two, three and four - joy, relief and discovery. Check.

However, he was not at the river's edge where Steve was, but at the end of the long green line, about ¼ mile back. I was excited to hear from someone who had so many details. I called Steve to tell him and planned to make the call the next day.

This was where it started to go South, and emotion numbers seven and eight - anger and rage - would come shortly into play.

I phoned him the next day and we talked for nearly an hour. I explained some things that Steve had told me and he filled in some big blanks. He asked me to send him the chapter we'd written about the river. We finished our conversation and said we'd talk the next day. I sent the chapter that afternoon and the next day waited for the call.

Instead of a phone call, I received a scathing email from him. Apparently the night before, he'd called up a couple of his old friends and told them about our conversation.

Now as I mentioned before, my conversations with certain veterans ranged from "No, that didn't happen" to "Yeah, that happened and let me tell you about my story." Confusion was there, to say the least.

I'd sent him the chapter about the river. I'd told him about Special Projects, the Ashau, Agent Orange and Steve's blank DD-214 (which Steve and I always called "blacked out"). His email response accused Steve and me of lying. He said that Steve should have known the name of the hamlet during Pacification. He stated he'd seen Agent Orange being sprayed, and the way Steve described it was incorrect. He claimed that we were lying about Steve's empty DD-214. Hotel was never in the Ashau (HELLO - Dewey Canyon was IN THE ASHAU). The CIA never controlled contraband in Vietnam. Steve never received the Navy Commendation Medal. He said that grunts over there never referred to their squad by name (meaning 3-Charlie squad). He even stated that he wasn't even sure that Agent Orange was the true cause for killing so many veterans. He referred to our book as one giant "sea story".

And guess what he asked me at the end of the email?

"You and Steve coming to the reunion this summer?"

Are you kidding me?

Emotion number seven - anger. Check.

Now, I should have left well enough alone at this point. But I was angry. *Extremely* angry. I can understand someone not wanting to talk about their time in Vietnam, but to totally deny events ever took place? To deny reality even with proof of things?

So I picked up the phone and called him. He was very calm and so was I, but he could tell I was angry, and he played on it. "If your story is real, then why are you so angry?" Well, I don't like Steve being called a liar.

After I said that, he said he didn't even think Steve existed – even though I'd also sent him 8-10 pictures with Steve clearly in the center of the shot! He informed me that he was a retired police officer, and that his "police instincts" were telling him I was lying about everything. He said he felt that the whole thing was a set up on my part, and that I was attempting something "devious" that he couldn't put his finger on. I told him that if his police senses were telling him that something was wrong, then he was probably a piss-poor cop when he was on the force. The conversation ended.

So I researched his name and found out that he now worked within the V.A. Wow, did the light bulb ever go off. Couple that with Steve's CUE case (where they're denying these very same events ever took place) and you've got a grunt who became a turncoat and was now one of the Vulture Assassins. It made sense. I emailed him, letting him know that I knew he worked for the V.A. I advised him to check Steve's DD-214 himself, since I knew he had access to it there. I also emailed him a copy of the

Navy Commendation Medal document. I reminded him that if he was in fact a part of Operation Dewey Canyon as he'd admitted before, then he himself was in the Ashau, as it part of the OFFICIAL MISSION STATEMENT - and the official documents included admissions that they were IN LAOS as part of that mission.

A month passed with no response.

Finally, out of the blue was an email in my inbox from him. In it, he admitted that Steve was in fact real (duh) and the medal document was valid. He did get hold of Steve's

DD-214, but blamed the gaps on a clerical error. He stood firm on the rest of his points

(The Ashau, The CIA, Agent Orange) and advised me to read a book called "Stolen Valor". Emotion number eight - rage. Check.

I never responded and I've not heard from him again. I hope I never do.

My journey for documentation continued, as Steve and I both knew NBC was there at the river that day. Steve and I talked about how cool it would be to see that footage if it still existed. So together, we decided to see what we could do to get our hands on it.

Neither one of us was optimistic. But I forged ahead.

I sat down on a Saturday and emailed NBC's newsroom. I gave them specifics, including the date and location and I let them know that I was certain NBC was there. I fully expected not to hear back from anyone. I was surprised when I received a call that following Monday from a young lady in the archive department. She let me know that it would probably take three months to find it, as they had several places where they kept the archives – and it would cost me significantly if the footage was found. Later that day, she dropped me an email and referred me to the Department of Defense – informing me that NBC had turned over all their footage to them in the mid-70s. She provided me with a contact email at the DOD. So I emailed them all the details (date, location, mission name, etc.), asking for mission details as well, knowing full well I'd never hear a peep.

Surprisingly, I did and rather quickly I might add. I received a call from a woman at the Pentagon and the Spanish Inquisition began again. This time, I was a little bit more reserved, as I informed her that my father-in-law was there and really wanted to see exactly what happened that day. Her words shocked me more than anyone else I'd spoken to:

"That documentation related to the Phoenix Program is still classified."

Wait a second.

I didn't mention the Phoenix Program.

There was a long pause on my end.

"Ma'am, I'm not looking for any documents related to Phoenix. I just want a copy of that footage for my own research." Another long pause.

"That's classified."

I began laughing into the phone. I think she realized her mistake in giving me confirmation without even knowing it. Then it hit her.

"Have a nice day, sir."

Click.

My body began to get warm. You know, when your adrenaline kicks in - the fight or flight syndrome? I was warm all over. I had found my answer.

It was true. Phoenix was there that day. Perhaps as a joint operation with 2/3/3 under the guise of Operation Prairie Fire? I do not know, and frankly at this point, I do not care. It explained Steve's lower ranked medal. It explained why the men killed received posthumous high ranking medals. They couldn't tell their story. It confirmed the statement from the veteran about Special Projects, Phoenix and CIA involvement. It explained Steve's side, since he'd described to me how the intel that day was so pinpoint. In explained why they were in Laos, instead of near Khe Sahn, like the official dossier stated.

It explained everything. And forty-two years later, it's still being covered up and denied.

And I'm still as confused as ever.

I think the big things I've learned throughout this journey are that everyone has their own view of the events that transpired in Vietnam. Some saw and committed atrocities and others didn't. That didn't mean they didn't happen. Some were sprayed with Agent Orange and others weren't. That doesn't mean it didn't happen. Some veterans have PTSD. Some don't. That doesn't mean it's not real. I still don't know why prior veterans turned their backs on the Vietnam vet. I don't think I'll ever have a definitive answer. The V.A. system is broken in so many ways. It needs to be fixed. I don't ever see that happening. Every veteran has his story. Much can be confirmed by eyewitness accounts and limited proof with existing fragmented documentation. But there will still be detractors and accusers. Many of those detractors are veterans themselves who either don't want to or cannot face reality. Traitors still exist. Many of them work at the Veteran's Administration. Many are veterans themselves.

It's truly disheartening. But I am encouraged never the less by what you've read in this book. My hope is that if you are a veteran, or if you are facing your "Three Words" moment, this book has touched your heart and let you know that someone is listening. Someone is watching. Someone cares and is waiting for you to cry out and receive your visitation. Emotion number three – joy. Check.

Perhaps I went into this journey with a sense of arrogance or visions of grandeur. Perhaps I thought I could just research, make phone calls, write letters and everything would just fall into my lap.

God Help Me for thinking that.

BONUS LETTERS

Letter from Gonzalez to Kay Mitchell, Mother of Steven R. Mitchell

Note: In the Nam, at first writing letters were a means to communicate with the outside world. Things go south rapidly in this jungle war. Gonzales would cover for me by writing letters to my mother. "Everything is fine" is what Gonzalez used. The turning point was when he sent home to my parent's a picture of me eating my lunch at the top of a pile of enemy soldiers. We were hit by waves trying to overrun perimeter. The order of business was to drag all the bodies to one location, look for documents, stack their weapon`s I decided this was a perfect photo shoot at the top putting their heads under each arm- now snap it. "Dear Mom & Dad, keep these pictures after you develop them for me."

I was numb and not thinking about the impact of their son who they knew no more, years later I regretted hurting them!

Steve Mitchell

Gonzalez letter to Kay Mitchell, mother of Steven R. Mitchell

Dear Kay,

I hope you and your family are in the best of health. We are all fine. I felt pretty bad when you told me you haven`t heard from Steve for over a week, but don`t worry he is all right. I haven`t see him for quite some time, but I know he is fine, i always have ways of finding out about him and the other guys. You see, sometimes they are so busy, running patrols, etc., etc. And when they come back to the area, they`re so tired that all they wanna do is lay down and sleep it off. Where I`m at we have it a lot easier.

We don`t run too many patrols and none of that jazz. So please don`t worry too much about him, he is fine.

I`m sure glad some people had fun on Valentine`s day. I didn`t. No even a card from my girl. Well, I guess she is having a ball down there so probably she figures I'm having fun down here, so maybe that's why she didn`t bother. Like Mike, I also had a bad experience with a girl, not the one I'm going with now but the one before that. I trusted her blindly. I had so much faith in her she wrong did me, hurt me so bad that`s the main reason why I`m here. Just because a girl hurt my pride.

Oh well, let me not engage you with my problems after all that belongs to the past. My cousin, the one Steve's writing to is it her name is Geno. Steve and I are planning to go to Bangkok for R+R. We are going to take it on April. I just hope we can go at the same time. I don`t really have plans when I get out of the service. Probably I'll go to college or maybe I'll just go back to work at the same office where I used to work before I came to the service. It all depends. Well, this will be all for today. Take care and God bless you all.

Love,

Junior

Note: Gonzalez Letter

Junior Gonzalez, my best friend came home with PTSD

In the 90`s Junior committed suicide.

Run his truck head on into train.

Rest in Honor Junior.

Letter to Mike Mitchell, older brother

AUG?

Dear Mike,

Hi! How you been? Just fine, I hope! I sure was glad to get your letter! I am sorry I haven`t written sooner but live been so busy. Well tell Mom & Dad I'm fine; I only have time for one letter so I'm writing you because you leaving soon. Tell Mom + Dad I'm sorry about not writing but I don`t have time right now. Well, the last 10 or more days I've been up on Dong Ha Mountain. It`s close to the DMZ. I hope you`ve been having a good time while you are home. I sure wish I could see your car. I always dreamed of having a Road runner. What color is it? Mike when you get to your next duty station write and send me your address. I`ll write you as often as I can. Mike it`s not necessary for you to send me a package you haven't got that much time. Thanks a lot anyway. Tell Mom + Dad when they send ma a package, I need writing paper + pen real soon. In their package I'd like cans of fruit cookies and 1 small bottle of Worcestershire sauce. That sauce is for a good friend of mine. Explain to Granny that I can`t write for a while, well Mom wanted to know what my schedule is, what I am doing etc. Well, I'm going on patrols during the day. I go on LP, a listening post at night at least five night a week/ that's really hell/ somedays I go on O.P out posts, I just search for Gooks then.

A few days ago, I spotted Gooks down in the valley, this Lieutenant let me call in the fire mission. We really messed up quite a few Gooks.

I called in 105 H.W. Rounds. Well finally tomorrow I'm leaving for Camp Carrol.

I sure am glad, they`ve been hitting us with rockets, mortars about every night. Mike I sure was sorry to hear your friend Chris was killed, I know how you feel. I was glad to hear you got home safe. I was so relieved because I sure did worry about you when you were over here. I tell you Mike this is a hell of a war. I`ve got a lot of respect for NVA, but I love killing them. They fight a hard war. The other day we found some Marines after the Gooks got through with them. I`ll never forget what they did to them. It goes two ways though.

I sure am glad you got to meet Holly she`s a real nice girl isn't she. Mike how is the family. Tell all the kids Hi for me. Tell Mom I got a letter from Becky Kinley the other day. Tell her I'll write her soon. Tell Rick+ Debbie T. Hi! For me.

I`m sure glad we`re going to Camp Carrol there's Gooks all around us. I should be writing a few more letter`s when I get to Carrol. At Carrol I'll be doing is going on mine sweeps the word is pretty soon our company is going down south to around Danang. I don't know whether I like that idea or not. There`s quite a few booby traps down South+NVA.

Well Mike take care of yourself. Tell Mom +Dad, I'll write them as soon as i can. Tell Holly I'll write her to tell Granny thanks for the Kool-Aid and gum in her letters. Well, I sure miss the family you to. Well write me soon. Tell Mom+ Dad to write me to have a good time.

LOVE

STEVE

P.S. Sure love+miss all of you.

For more information and pictures and
TV appearances by Steve:
Go to GodHelpMeTheBook.com

Made in the USA
Middletown, DE
02 September 2024